L
O
N
D
O
N

LONDON

LOUISE NICHOLSON

PHOTOGRAPHS
RICHARD TURPIN

FRANCES LINCOLN

For Nick, who has shared all my London years. L.N.

Frances Lincoln Limited
4 Torriano Mews
Torriano Avenue
London NW5 2RZ

London
Copyright © Frances Lincoln 1998
Text copyright © Louise Nicholson 1998
Photographs copyright © Richard Turpin 1998

The right of Louise Nicholson to be identified
as the author of this Work has been asserted by
her in accordance with the Copyright, Design
and Patents Act 1988 (UK).

The right of Richard Turpin to be identified as
the photographer of this Work has been
asserted by him in accordance with the
Copyright, Design and Patents Act 1988 (UK).

British Library Cataloguing-in-publication data.
A catalogue record for this book is available from the
British Library.

ISBN 0-7112-1187-6

Set in Legacy by Frances Lincoln Limited
Printed and bound in Italy by Conti Tipocolor
First Frances Lincoln edition April 1998

9 8 7 6 5 4 3 2 1

PAGE 1 *Goodwin's Court, a narrow alley lined
with Georgian houses, links Covent Garden with
St Martin's Lane.*

PAGES 2-3 *Old and new markets vie for
space in the City. Here, Leadenhall food market
is juxtaposed with Richard Rogers' Lloyd's
insurance building.*

ABOVE *At night, the grey Portland stone façade of
the Royal Society of Painters in Watercolours
building on Piccadilly is bathed in purple light.*

RIGHT *Alfred Gilbert's aluminium* Angel of
Christian Charity, *better known as* Eros, *honours
the 7th Earl of Shaftesbury, a Victorian
philanthropist and statesman.*

CONTENTS

THE RIVER THAMES

FROM WESTMINSTER TO THE THAMES BARRIER

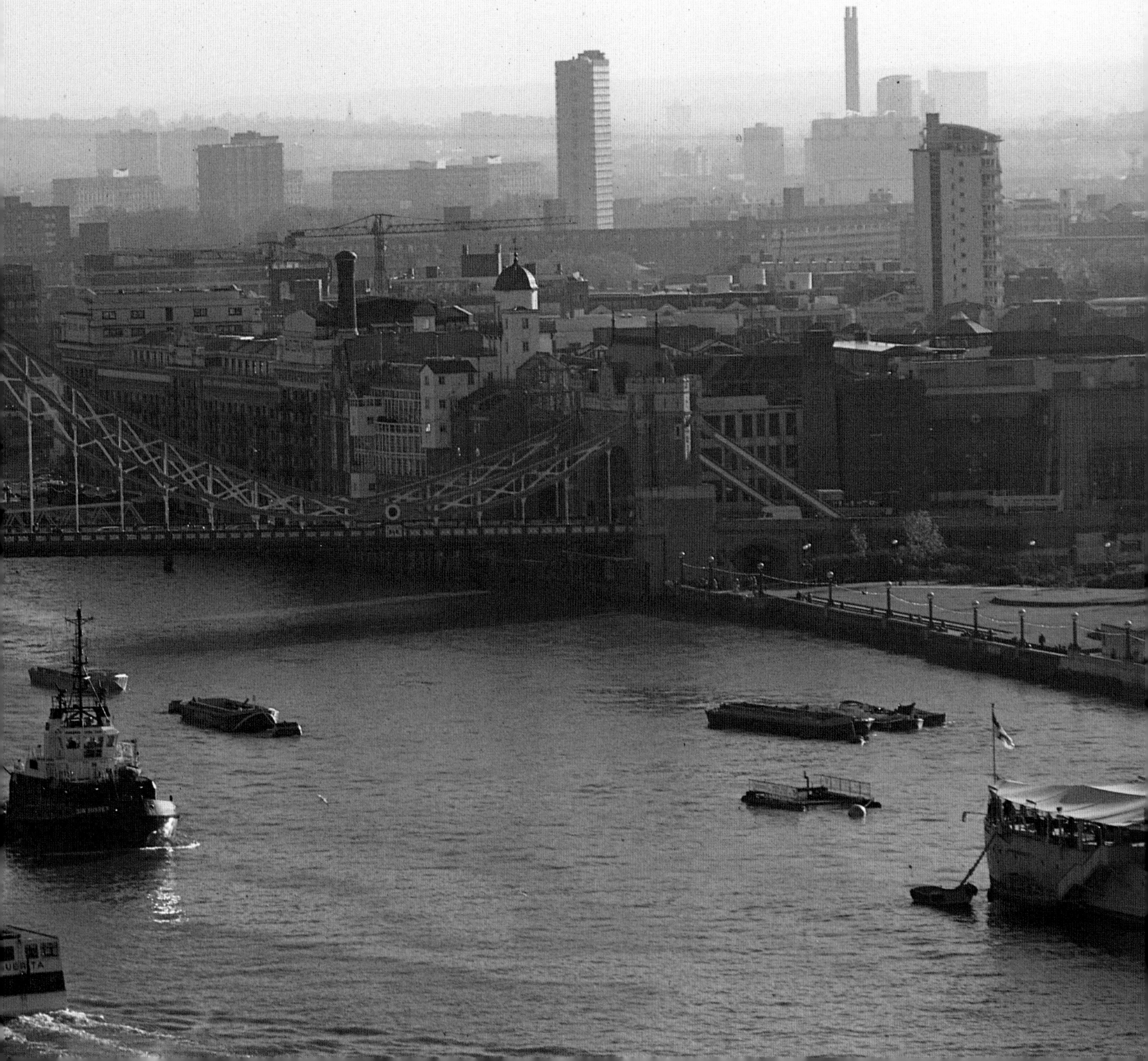

'The old river on its broad reach unrolled at the decline of day
after ages of good service done to the race that people its bank
. . . spread out in the tranquil dignity of a waterway leading to
the uttermost ends of the earth . . . It has known and served all
the men of whom the nation is proud – the adventurers and the
settlers . . . hunters for gold or pursuers of fame, they had all
gone out on that stream, bearing the sword, and often the torch,
messengers of the might within the land, bearers of the spark
from sacred fire. What greatness had not floated on the ebb of
that river into the mystery of an unknown earth . . . The
dreams of men, the seed of commonwealth, the germs of empires.'

Joseph Conrad, who wrote these words in 1902 in his novel *Heart of Darkness*, was a Polish immigrant who became a master seaman before turning to writing. He was just the man to capture the constancy, the greatness and the romance of the Thames at the height of its 'good service'. Rising among the hills and villages of Gloucestershire, Britain's longest river snakes its way eastwards across England, to empty into the North Sea. As it twists and turns for 20 miles (32 km) through the vastness of London, its waters lap against the buildings, docks and bridges that tell the capital's story.

This story began when the Thames basin was a wild, forested and uncultivated land, regularly flooded with tidal surges. Bronze and Iron Age traders used the river as their highway to the Continent, sailing down it and across the sea to the Rhine. In 54 BC, Julius Caesar arrived from Gaul and travelled by land to the spot where London now stands, where the Thames was still tidal but could easily be crossed. Once he had defeated the local tribesmen he left.

A century later, in AD 43, the Romans returned with a greater force. Under the Emperor Claudius, an army of 40,000 forded the Thames and secured the north bank, making it the link between Colchester, the capital of their new province, and the Kent ports. Londinium, as they called it, was well situated. Not far from the sea, the Thames here was deep enough for a port while the north bank was protected by two flat-topped hills with a marsh behind and a river, the Walbrook, to the west. Trade flourished.

When the British tribes rebelled in AD 61 and the defiant Queen Boudicca led them in the destruction first of Colchester, then of

Londinium, Roman forces promptly rebuilt their burgeoning port.

By AD 70, the Thames had its first London Bridge. It led to Southwark, the Romans' military supply base and London's earliest suburb. Towards the end of the second century, the port was enlarged with a 600-yard- (550-m-) long quay, and by about the year 200 Londinium had a strong defensive wall. It became the hub of the Romans' impressive road system and the sophisticated capital of the Roman province. Ships arrived with dried fruit from Palestine, marble from Turkey and Greece, oil from Spain, amber from the Baltic, wine from Italy – and sometimes pirates.

In 410, with their empire dwindling, the Romans left. Londinium declined, but the port's continuing wealth attracted invaders. Among these were the Vikings. Sailing up the Thames in their dragon-prowed ships, they came repeatedly in the ninth and tenth centuries, to be ousted first by the Christian Saxon king Alfred (who ruled 871-99), then by Aethelred II ('The Unready', who ruled 978-1016).

But in 1016, the young Danish Viking, Canute, was proclaimed King of all England and made London his capital. This City of London became the trading centre of an increasingly unified England. Its international prestige soared, its population exploded, and soon wharves lined the waterfront from what is now Blackfriars Bridge almost to the Tower of London.

The arrival of the Normans signalled the rise of the City of Westminster, 2½ miles (4 km) upstream from the City of London. After William the Conqueror crushed King Harold at the Battle of Hastings in 1066, he marched to London, burning Southwark and destroying crops in his wake until the people offered him the crown. He established himself at Westminster, the site of a palace built by an earlier English king, Edward the Confessor. Now Westminster became the seat of royal and state power, while downstream in the City the merchants held sway.

In the following centuries, the Thames would be central to the spectacular rise of both the royal City of Westminster and the merchants' City of London – the two eventually combining to form the London we know today.

Viewed from the Monument, this panorama down the Thames (previous page) shows HMS Belfast, *Tower Bridge and south London stretching beyond. Upstream, the Houses of Parliament (left) gain a new romance at sunset when seen across the water from Westminster Bridge.*

CLEANING UP THE THAMES

George Vulliamy's Sphinx (left), erected in 1882 to flank Cleopatra's Needle, and a mooring ring (right) decorate Victoria Embankment. The three embankments – Victoria (1864-70), Albert (1866-9) and Chelsea (1871-4) – were all built on land reclaimed from the Thames. They were engineered by the genius Sir Joseph Bazalgette, who had been called in to address the problem of the pollution of the Thames, which had become steadily worse over the centuries.

As London grew, so the waters of the Thames became increasingly unhygienic and sluggish. In winter, they would often freeze up completely, a disaster mitigated only by the jolly frost fairs with bull-baiting, horse-racing and football matches staged on the ice. In summer, the water gave off such a terrible stench that Parliament could barely sit. Thanks to the more than 300 sewers emptying into the Thames, the drinking water was contaminated and between the 1840s and 1860s there were regular epidemics. In 1848-9 a cholera epidemic claimed 13,000 lives. In 1858, the Great Stink caused by the dry hot summer became a national issue.

The Thames, with its lucrative tax revenues, had been administered by the City Corporation since 1197, when Richard I handed over the rights in return for cash to finance his crusades. In 1857, Queen Victoria's lawyers won it back. The following year, Parliament passed a Bill for the Purification of the Thames, and in 1859, the Metropolitan Board of Works commissioned Bazalgette to solve the problem. His solution was to reclaim strips of land by the river to make it narrower, so that it would flow more swiftly and not freeze up. He used this land for a trunk sewer to take London's effluent out of town, a road to relieve the congested Strand, water and gas conduits and telegraph lines, an underground railway line and public gardens.

From earliest times, the river had been the city's main highway. For most Londoners, the fastest way to move across the city was to take a boat. 'Up by 4 a-clock and at 5 by water to Woolwich, there to see the manner of tarring', the diarist Samuel Pepys noted in 1661; 'By water to the Strand and so to the King's playhouse'; and again, 'Up and by water to Whitehall, and there with the Duke of York did our usual business.'

The Thames was also a choice place for aristocrats to set up home. Watergates led to their riverside mansions along the Strand. One that survives is York Watergate, originally part of the home of Charles I's favourite, the Duke of Buckingham.

For the royals, the Thames provided the link between their many riverside palaces as well as an airy backdrop to the pageantry that expressed their power. From the busy city, royal barges accompanied by boatloads of courtiers made their stately progress up- and downriver, drawing crowds as the party moved from one palace to another. The diarist John Evelyn watched Charles II return from his coronation in Westminster Abbey in 1660: 'Crowne Imperial on his head ... to Westminster Stayres where he tooke Water in a Triumphal barge to White-hall where was extraordinary feasting.' It was for another royal river event in about 1715 that Handel wrote his Water Music for George I. In 1806, amid great pomp, Nelson's body was brought from Greenwich to Whitehall stairs by water, then taken through the streets for burial at St Paul's Cathedral.

The merchants of the City enjoyed their pageantry, too. From 1422 to 1856, the increasingly splendid annual parade of City Livery Companies' gilded barges took the Lord Mayor-elect to Westminster for the sovereign's ritual approval. In 1452 the Mayor launched a new barge with silver oars, but extravagance reached even greater heights in the sixteenth and seventeenth centuries. For Thomas Middleton's journey in 1613, a fleet of Livery Company barges, each decorated with its coat of arms, followed the glistening boat carrying the Lord Mayor-elect past five specially built islands decorated with Indian fruit trees, spices and a fairy castle. Even today, though the Lord Mayor's parade takes place on land, the celebrations end with a spectacular fireworks display over the Thames – as if to commemorate the extravagant riverside displays of the past.

Seen from Westminster Bridge, the City has a night-time beauty flattered by the river's garlands of bulbs and the glowing dome of St Paul's.

BLACKFRIARS BRIDGE TO THE TOWER

From Roman times until Westminster Bridge was opened in 1750, London had only one bridge, London Bridge. Grand watergates, simple stairs and precarious piers littered its banks. In the 1560s, there were thirty landing places between Westminster and the Tower. By 1827, when seven bridges had been built, maps plotted sixty-six river stairs between Battersea and the Isle of Dogs, and more than twenty piers.

The Thames of the nineteenth century cried out for help with its public transport. Ferries criss-crossed it relentlessly, carrying people, horses, carriages and cartloads of goods. Bridges at Blackfriars and Battersea followed that at Westminster, but these were not enough and it was not until the building of bridges at Waterloo, Southwark, Chelsea and Lambeth that the Thames began to be relieved of its acute congestion. The process was further assisted by the building of railway bridges bringing visitors and commuters right over the Thames into central London, to Charing Cross, Victoria, Broad Street and Cannon Street stations.

Joseph Cubitt's Blackfriars Bridge, with its five wrought iron arches (right), replaced an eighteenth-century bridge by Robert Mylne. Cubitt's bridge was opened in 1869 by Queen Victoria, who was so unpopular at the time the crowds hissed her.

Tower Bridge was built in the medieval style to fit in with the genuinely medieval Tower of London (overleaf). William the Conqueror began The Tower in the eleventh century, to keep a watch on the merchants of the City and to help protect London. It stood right by the merchants' port, between it and their lucrative trade routes. William lived well upstream, at Westminster, but some later monarchs – from King Stephen who came to the throne in 1135 to James I who died in 1625 – enlarged the Tower and chose to live there. Others, such as Princess Elizabeth, later Elizabeth I, arrived through Traitors' Gate as prisoners.

London's river trade increased during the sixteenth and seventeenth centuries. The busiest section was that around the City of London. Cloth, for instance, was shipped from here to the Netherlands, Russia, the Baltic and Turkey, while English adventurers and traders returned from India and China with silks and spices, and from America with tobacco and sugar.

By the end of the eighteenth century, London was the largest port in the world – and a paradise for smugglers and thieves. At any one time, some 8,000 boats of all sizes and types might be crammed into the 6-mile (10-km) stretch of dockland, 2 miles (3 km) of them upstream from London Bridge. The worst chaos was at Upper Pool, just below London Bridge, where ships fought for mooring space. Those anchored midstream had their cargo unloaded by lightermen and dumped on the quay where it might be left unguarded for weeks. An estimated half of all cargo simply disappeared. To counteract this, in 1798 the City merchants founded the River Police, armed with cutlasses and blunderbusses. The world's oldest police force, it still enforces river law today.

But the task of protecting cargoes from thieves and smugglers, and of alleviating the congestion of London's old docks, was not dealt with fully until the building of the enclosed docks in the nineteenth century. By then the Pool of London was struggling to cope with Britain's huge increase in trade, the result of its successful Industrial Revolution and its ever-growing Empire.

The enclosed docks were constructed piecemeal by private companies on the flat land east of the City. First came the West India Docks, covering 54 acres (22 hectares) of water and built by the West India Company. They opened in 1802 and were an instant success, cutting the time needed for merchants to discharge their cargoes from four weeks to four days. Other enclosed docks quickly followed, among them the London Docks (1805) and Thomas Telford's 23-acre (9-hectare) St Katharine's Dock (1828). The vast Royal Docks complex came last. Eleven miles (17 km) long and covering 245 acres (100 hectares), this consisted of the Royal Victoria (1855), the Royal Albert (1880) and the King George V Docks (1921). With their surrounding markets, the Royal Docks soon became a magnet for migrant workers and immigrants.

St Katharine's Dock opened in 1828. Having closed in 1968, in the 1970s it became the first of the old docks to be rehabilitated.

Before the enclosed docks came to the east of the City, the area was sprinkled with small villages. At Shadwell on the north bank, sailors and boatmen lived among the roperies, tanneries and taverns. Captain Cook stayed here in the eighteenth century between his three expeditions to the Pacific. Limehouse, renowned for its clean air and lime kilns, became a shipbuilding centre and, in the eighteenth century, home to London's first Chinese immigrants who ran the exotic opium and gambling dens, as visited by Oscar Wilde's desperate Dorian Gray. Downstream, the Isle of Dogs' marshy meadows and cornfields were once drained by windmills.

On the south bank, Rotherhithe was the site of Edward III's palace. Here his son, the Black Prince, fitted out a fleet of ships for an invasion of France. Later, in 1620, Captain Jones set sail from Rotherhithe, bound for the New World in the Pilgrim Fathers' boat *The Mayflower*. At neighbouring Deptford, Henry VIII built a Royal Dock or 'King's Yard' for his navy in 1513; and Elizabeth I knighted Sir Francis Drake after he circumnavigated the world in his ship the *Golden Hind*.

Greenwich, further downstream, was the heart of London's naval life and provided the inspiration for much of its scientific leadership. The proof may be seen in its hilltop Royal Observatory, its National Maritime Museum, and its position on the Meridian Line and at the centre of world time.

Beyond Greenwich, the Thames widens along the Greenwich and Blackwall reaches. It was from Blackwall on the north bank that John Smith and the Virginia Settlers left in 1616 to found the first permanent colony in America. And it was here, in the nineteenth century, that the large ships of the powerful East India Company docked and the *Cutty Sark* unloaded her precious China tea.

Further east along the south bank beyond Busby's Reach is Woolwich, where Henry VIII built his first Royal Dockyard in 1512. The *Great Harry*, the largest ship of its day and the flagship of Henry's navy, was constructed in this year. The docks were to impress Daniel Defoe in the 1720s as 'exceeding spacious and convenient; and are also prodigious full of all manner of stores of timber, plank, masts, pitch, tar and all manner of naval provisions'.

From the City, the view south-east takes in delicate City spires and the soaring elegance of Canary Wharf Tower.

With the arrival of container ships, the enclosed docks became obsolete. In 1982, the Port of London moved out to Tilbury and the great docks, which had employed two million people when the Empire was at its peak, fell silent. Riverside buildings had once presented their finest façades to the river, but for a few years London would turn its back on its lifeblood.

For a while it had a mere token of river life: a ferry between the Tower and HMS *Belfast*, a Royal Navy cruiser now open to the public; dredgers clearing up silt; the River Police out on the beat; sailing boats at Richmond; motor yachts riding out from St Katharine's Dock and public pleasure boats plying the routes between the few surviving piers.

The river's revival began in the late 1980s and now Londoners have returned to living beside the Thames, whether in converted warehouses or in dramatic contemporary buildings such as Piers Gough's Cascades flats on the Isle of Dogs. Old riverside buildings have been given new life – the London Aquarium is housed in one by Westminster Bridge and Sir Terence Conran has put a clutch of restaurants in disused warehouses by Tower Bridge. The marshy south bank east of Greenwich is also being regenerated. The Thames is even to have a new bridge, the only new span to be built in the twentieth century, linking the City with Bankside.

The Royal Docks complex has given way to the London City Airport, which provides visitors from Europe with an airport close to the City of London. For local people, there is waterskiing, sailing, canoeing, windsurfing, motorcycle training and, at the London Arena, sports events, concerts, exhibitions and light entertainment.

Near here, the great metal fins of the Thames Barrier, built 1975-82 and the world's largest movable flood barrier, rise out of the water. They close the river off from its sea routes, protecting London from the perilous high tides which threaten to flood the city as it sinks slowly but steadily into its clay foundations.

The water of the river has been cleaned up too. Dace, whiting, flounder, herring, the fussy salmon and a hundred other species of fish have been spotted recently. Gap sites are being used to add to Greater London's impressive count of 67 square miles (175 square km) of parkland, while along the towpaths and in patches of wetlands sightings of snipe and lapwing, and blossoming celandine and marsh ragwort evoke the wild, uncultivated land the Thames watered when London's story began.

'June 2. A large Whale taken . . . which drew an infinite Concourse to see it, by water, horse, coach, on foote from Lond, and all parts: It appeared first below Greenewich at low-water, . . . after a long Conflict it was killed with the harping yrons, and struck in the head . . . and after a horrid grone it ran quite on shore and died.'

John Evelyn, *Diary,* 1658

The revitalized Docklands (above) are an exciting cocktail of water, industrial cranes and sparkling new buildings. They and the rest of London are protected from floods by the gleaming fins of the Thames Barrier (right) which lower when water runs dangerously high.

THE MERCHANTS' CITY AND PORT

THE CITY OF LONDON, DOCKLANDS AND THE EAST END

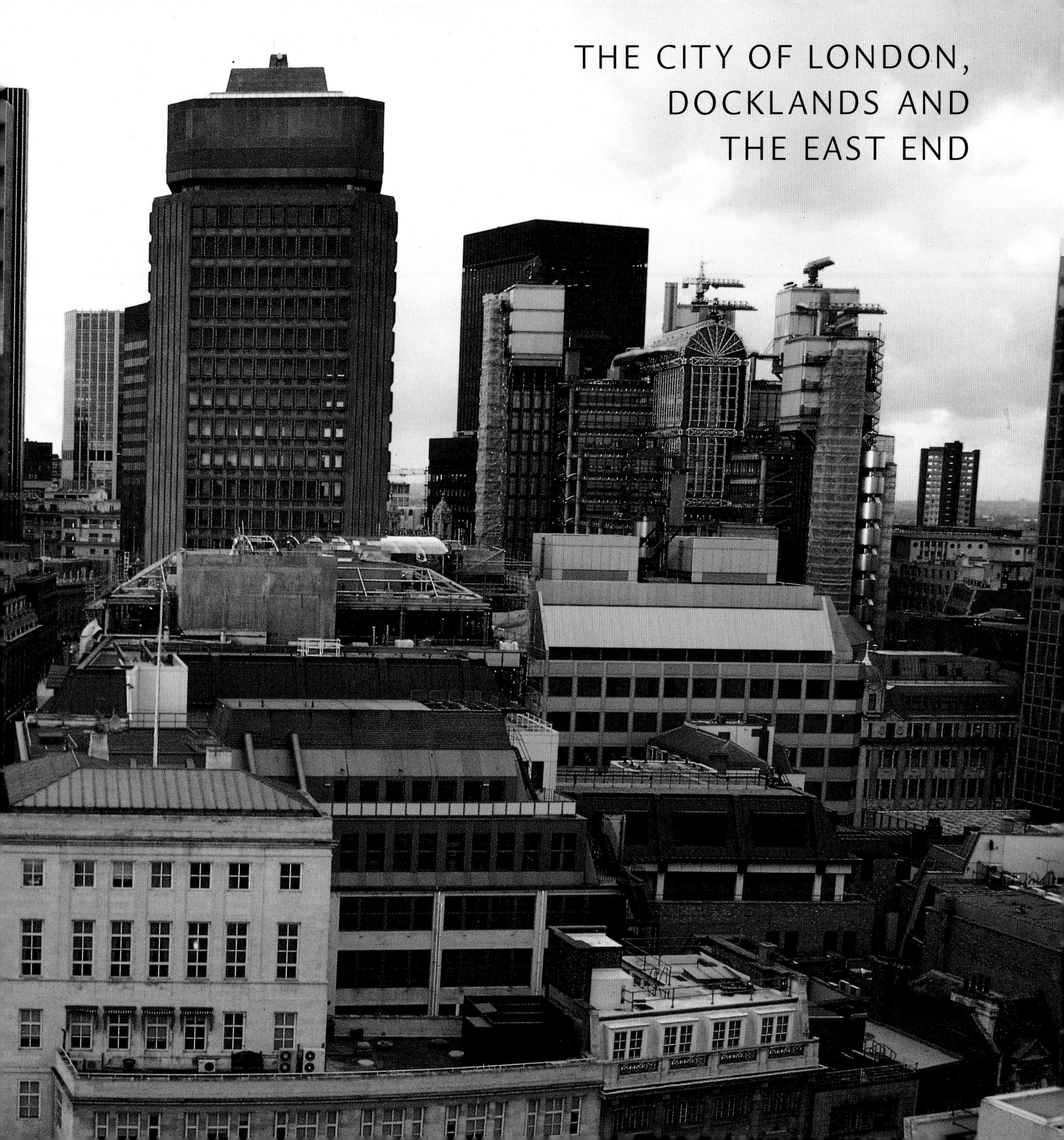

'There is no place in the town which I so much love to frequent as the Royal Exchange. It gives me a
secret satisfaction, and in some measure gratifies my vanity, as I am an Englishman, to see so rich an assembly
of countrymen and foreigners, consulting together upon the private business of mankind, and making this
metropolis a kind of emporium for the whole earth.'

Addison, the essayist and politician, was writing about the Royal Exchange in *The Spectator* in 1711, when London was at its peak. With a population that had shot up from 50,000 in 1530 to 200,000 by the end of that century, then soared again to 575,000 by 1700, it was the wonder of Europe. The City merchants had made London a honeypot for all to drink from.

Its port handled 80 per cent of England's imports and 69 per cent of its exports. London's commerce was its lifeblood and Addison was justified in feeling its commercial heartbeat most strongly in the Royal Exchange, that symbol of Tudor commercial success.

The Roman origins of this success are still evident today. After Queen Boudicca had destroyed Londinium in AD 61, the Romans rebuilt it and made it the capital of their British province. Around the year 200, they encircled it with a stone and brick wall 2 miles (3 km) long and 20 feet (6 m) high. Fragments of wall, some with medieval additions, survive on the periphery of the City, around the Barbican, in Noble Street and in the Tower of London. Today, the location of lost gateways can be found in street names such as Ludgate and Bishopsgate.

Inside this prosperous city, low-rise, red-tiled houses lined wide, straight streets such as Watling Street, an offshoot of the Dover–St Alban's road. These led past public baths, villas, gardens and temples to the huge central Forum and Basilica that straddled what is today Gracechurch Street, London's central marketplace and business area.

Many Roman finds, from the Temple of Mithras in Victoria Street to sunken ships, help give a picture of a city where about 60,000 inhabitants enjoyed a sophisticated life in villas equipped with glass windows, heating and running water.

Trade continued after the Romans left, but this attracted invaders. One was the Saxon and Christian king of Wessex, Alfred, who took the city in 886 and renamed it Lundenwix. A century of prosperity followed, during which scholarship was encouraged, a code of law devised, texts were translated into the vernacular and monasteries were founded. Christianity had already arrived in 604 when Mellitus, a monk from Rome, was ordained Bishop of London and the small wooden church of St Paul's was built on London's west hill. Fire and destruction would claim four churches on this spot before Sir Christopher Wren built his Baroque masterpiece, completed in 1710.

When the Viking, Canute, took this city, England's largest and wealthiest, in 1016, he made it capital of all England, improved the country's administration and set up a formidable fiscal policy that enabled him to levy more taxes in real terms than most other English rulers until the seventeenth century.

On this foundation, the medieval London of the merchants prospered. The city was impressive. Inside its stone walls with seven double gateways and towers, the bells of about 140 church spires and

City skyscrapers (previous page) stand among vestiges of the City's earlier history – a chunk of Roman wall (above)
and the Royal Exchange's gilded grasshopper (above right).

towers rang out gaily through the narrow streets, rising above the flimsy, multi-storey, wood and plaster houses. And in 1176, a succession of wooden London Bridges was replaced by Peter de Colechurch's stone one, soon to be cluttered with a mass of multi-storeyed wooden houses.

With England becoming increasingly unified, both national and international trade soared. And as the City merchants' coffers filled, so their power over the Norman and Plantagenet kings at Westminster increased. Each time a king came, cap in hand for money for crusades or wars, the City gave just enough but demanded more privileges in return. Henry I gave the City merchants the right to collect their own taxes, Richard I gave up the lucrative management of the Thames, and finally, in 1215, King John had to agree that the elected Mayor of London symbolized the City's independence from Westminster. Even today, the City's perimeters are clearly marked by a statue of a gryphon rampant, the unofficial badge of the City, and the sovereign has to ceremoniously ask permission to enter.

The merchants ruled the City. Taking little account of democracy, they created a new class – that of citizen. Citizenship could be bought, inherited or won after seven years' apprenticeship to another citizen. Two-thirds of Londoners were not eligible, including most foreigners and small traders.

The Mayor of London reinforced the system. He was elected annually by the aldermen, the representatives of the twenty-four wards or areas of the City, who were all wealthy merchants of the wool, cloth, fish, wine or other lucrative trades. The Mayor's Common Council fixed tolls for goods coming into the City from the rest of the country, and collected royal customs on foreign goods. To tighten its hold on trade, it decreed that provincial and foreign traders could only sell to, or through, a citizen of London, and could only stay in London for forty days. Small traders got around these rules and the hefty tolls that were charged to enter the City by setting up their markets outside the City gates.

As the merchants and bankers flourished under the City's regime, so did the craftsmen who founded guilds to maintain standards and protect their interests. A guild member might become a liveryman, the first step on the ladder leading to citizenship, alderman and the top position – Lord Mayor. The best known of these was Richard, or Dick, Whittington, a mercer who rose to become a silk supplier to the king. He was three times Master of the Mercers' Company and, between 1397 and 1419, four times Mayor. During Whittington's lifetime, the City fathers began building the Guildhall (1411-40), whose medieval crypt is London's largest. Upstairs, in its new Hall, the City's continuing influence is still officially acknowledged when the prime minister of the day accounts for government policy in a speech given each year at the Lord Mayor's Banquet.

By the early sixteenth century, London's merchants badly needed somewhere new to do business. Thomas Gresham, a merchant-financier and Lord Mayor, provided the solution in the shape of the Royal Exchange. When it opened for business in 1566 it significantly helped transfer the financial and trading capital of northern Europe from Antwerp to London, where it has remained ever since. Now London had Europe's finest purpose-built Bourse.

New trading houses began to climb the ladder of prosperity. The Baltic Exchange, which started towards the end of the seventeenth century on an informal basis in a coffee-house, is today the only international shipping exchange in the world. Lloyd's marine insurance, with similar origins, is the largest of its kind. The Bank of England, opened in 1694, originally raised money for the government to fund wars against France, and introduced the concept of a national debt. Today it helps keep London's financial markets at the forefront of Europe. More than 500 banks have their offices in the City, making it the centre for world banking. And the London Stock Exchange, which started trading in a Threadneedle coffee-house in the 1770s, is the most important stockmarket in Europe.

CITY STREET SIGNS

The Cutlers' Hall sign (right) hangs outside the Cutlers' livery hall in Warwick Lane. The cutlers – knife-makers or dealers – became an organized guild in the thirteenth century. As the prestige of medieval guilds such as this one grew, they bought land, built grand livery halls – among the finest are the Fishmongers' Hall and the Goldsmiths' Hall – and endowed churches, such as St Magnus Martyr, St Mary Abchurch and St Margaret Lothbury.

Today, the Cutlers' guild is one of the City Livery Companies. Their function is to protect and look after their members, to keep up standards, to control how many work at a craft or trade, and to control prices and wages as well as working conditions and welfare. Some companies, such as the Fishmongers', Mercers' and Leathersellers', are as old as the Cutlers'; others, such as the Arbitrators' and Chartered Accountants', have been founded to serve more modern professions.

Just as each guild gathered in one area, so did the bankers. The traditional street signs hanging in and around Lombard Street (left) all belong to bankers, many of whom came from Lombardy in northern Italy. Today, the City of London is the world's banking centre. Banks of all nationalities have offices here, and their buildings vary from ponderous Victorian symbols of reliability to the soaring NatWest tower which, at 600 feet (183 m), was, when completed in 1981, the world's tallest cantilevered building.

ST PAUL'S CATHEDRAL

In 1666, the Great Fire destroyed four-fifths of London, including 100 churches and 13,000 medieval wooden houses. 'It made me weep to see it,' wrote Pepys. 'The churches, houses, and all on fire and flaming at once, and a horrid noise the flames made, and the cracking of houses at their ruine.'

From now on, at Charles II's insistence, all new City building was to be in brick and stone and new streets, in contrast with the previous medieval huddle, were to be wide enough for people and transport to move along comfortably. Permission to build was given by the City Corporation which followed Parliament's Rebuilding Act of 1667. It was extremely comprehensive and dictated the rules governing foundations, joist sizes and the use of timber. (Building laws for the rest of London followed shortly.)

From the ashes of the Great Fire rose Sir Christopher Wren's St Paul's Cathedral, the graceful spires of his City churches, his Monument to the

Fire of London and many increasingly grand offices for the City merchants. This post-Fire City is the basis of the one we see today.

At the time of the Great Fire, Sir Christopher Wren was aged thirty-four. Three years later, while he was working on a grand scheme that had the new St Paul's at the centre of a network of bold wide boulevards, he was appointed the King's Surveyor-General. Nevertheless, the scheme was rejected by the clergy as being too radical. His second design – a dome on top of a Greek cross, the model of which now stands in the cathedral crypt – was again rejected as too modern. Finally, resorting to a design that he knew would please – one with a long nave – he won the clergy's approval, then quickly adapted it to shorten the nave, raise the walls, remove the spire from the dome (left) and add the monumental vestibule at the west end (far left and above). It is this design which we see today. The foundation stone was laid in 1675; the bulk of the work was completed by 1698, and Wren's son laid the last stone in 1710.

'I got into the heart of City life.
I saw and felt London at last . . .
I have seen the West-end, the parks,
the fine squares; but I love the City
far better. The City seems so much more
in earnest, its rush, its roar are such
serious things, sights, sounds. The City
is getting its living – the West-end but
enjoying its pleasures. At the West-end,
you may be amused, but in the City
you are excited.'

Charlotte Brontë, *Villette*, 1853

BUSY CITY LIFE

City workers emerge from Monument station (left). Many of them will do their lunchtime shopping in Sir Horace Jones's Leadenhall Market (right), built in 1881 off Gracechurch Street. It was restored to its colourful Victorian glory in the 1980s. Its iron and glazed arcades open on to a central space housing quality butchers, fishmongers, bakers, greengrocers and wine merchants. Standing on the site of a large Roman basilica, and nestling at the heart of the City's forest of skyscrapers, Leadenhall has survived all City clearances. The market began in the fourteenth century as a place where non-Londoners, known as 'foreigners', were permitted to sell their poultry. Cheese and butter were soon added; then it became a general market and sold leather and wool as well. After the Great Fire in 1666, it was rebuilt so that it was big enough to have special areas for selling a wider range of goods including raw hides, meat, fish, fruit and vegetables. Today's specialist, up-market shops are a microcosm of that great market.

THE MERCHANTS' CITY AND PORT

THE MEAT MARKET

Smithfield's livestock market (left), was the centre of meat-trading as early as the twelfth century, catering for London's increasing population. By the time Arnold Bennett knew it, it was far healthier than when Charles Dickens described it in *Oliver Twist*, published in 1837: 'The ground was covered, nearly ankle deep, with filth and mire; and thick steam perpetually rising from the reeking bodies of the cattle ...' In 1855, the sale of livestock was moved to Islington; only carcasses would be sold at Smithfield. Just over a decade later, Henry Jones's new market building opened, with its grand stone entrances (right) and four massive trading halls.

Outside the market stand four old telephone kiosks, until recently a familiar sight in London. 'Public call offices' were first sanctioned by the Postmaster General in 1884, the early ones usually being glazed wooden cabinets, rather like sentry boxes. By 1912 the General Post Office controlled most of the national telephone network and wanted a standardized design for its public call boxes. Of the various models that followed, Giles Gilbert Scott's of 1924 was the most successful. Known as the Kiosk No. 2 or K2, it was a fine example of British industrial design. As to its colour, Scott had originally suggested it be silver outside and 'greenish blue' inside.

'The ultimate interior had four chief colours: bright blue of the painted constructional ironwork, all columns and arches; red-pink-ivories of meat; white of the salesmen's long coats; and yellow of electricity ... One long avenue of bays stretched endless ... Many people in the avenues, loitering, chattering, chaffing ... market porters pushing trucks full of carcasses ...'

Arnold Bennett, *Imperial Palace*, 1930

A GEORGIAN ENCLAVE

The early eighteenth-century streets of
Spitalfields, hard by the City, have been
saved from neglect and avaricious developers
by a band of devoted conservationists who
have made many of the houses their homes.
They now form a protected and preserved
corner of inner London. Many were built by
Huguenot immigrants, French Protestants
who had fled religious persecution in France,
including those on Fournier Street (right)
which runs alongside Christ Church. Dating
from around 1722-8, some have large attic
windows that gave extra light for the
Huguenot weavers working at their silk looms.
A number of original decorative cantilevered
door cases survive, as do many of the unusual
exterior shutters.

Jewish and Bengali immigrants, with their
tailoring and mass-produced clothes-making
skills, succeeded the Huguenots in
Spitalfields, so the area continued to be a
ghetto for refugees as well as a home to the
textile trade. Among today's Bengali rag trade
factories and Asian shops and restaurants,
18 Folgate Street (left) stands especially
serene. Its owner has not only restored the
house, but has also furnished and decorated
some rooms in the style of the Huguenot
period, evoking the prosperity those silk
weavers brought to Spitalfields.

'Spitalfields, when I first came to live here in 1962, seemed to be caught in a time warp. The district had miraculously escaped the war-time bombing . . . The Georgian streets had been preserved by their poverty from improvement . . . weavers' attics no longer echoed to the clack of the loom, as they had done in the days when silk was the staple industry of the district, but the whirr of the sewing machine and the hiss of the pressing iron could still be heard from upstairs windows. In Fashion Street a forest of trade signs testified to the multiplicity of garment makers; the same was true of Hanbury Street, where tailors' workrooms competed for space with the fruit merchants, and Fournier Street, where Queen Anne houses, infinitely sub-divided, served as owner-occupied premises for the fur trade . . . Umbrella makers, a last vestige of the Spitalfields silk industry, were still to be found in obscure courtyards . . . '

Raphael Samuel, quoted in *The Saving of Spitalfields,* ed. Mark Girouard

While City merchants flourished, the area just outside the City – the East End – did not fare so well. The crisis came to a head in the late nineteenth century. By the time Queen Victoria celebrated her Jubilee in 1897, Britain was the world's richest country, its economy larger than those of France, Italy, Germany and Spain put together. But the price paid for this was the migration of thousands of British workers from a rural to an urban life. Overcrowding increased with the arrival in London of more than 100,000 Jews fleeing the pogroms of Russia and Poland.

Most of the migrants and immigrants settled in the East End, where housing was relatively cheap. Poverty and poor hygiene reached a nadir and life expectancy fell to an average of twenty-six years. While bawdy comedians and dancing girls provided escapism in the music halls of Shoreditch, inspired social workers such as Dr Barnardo and Charles Booth, founder of the Salvation Army, took to the streets of Bethnal Green, Whitechapel and Stepney in an effort to help the poor.

Today, Whitechapel's still relatively cheap accommodation has made it London's – indeed, Europe's – largest artists' colony, a dynamic force whose work is exhibited locally at the Whitechapel Art Gallery as well as in Mayfair and worldwide.

The second half of the twentieth century has brought more changes to the City and the East End than at any time since the Great Fire. First, the Blitz of the Second World War destroyed two-thirds of it. The Barbican, with its offices, flats and cultural centre, first proposed in 1956, was the idealistic, high-rise start to post-war rebuilding. Second, the use of deep-water container ships forced the Port of London to move to Tilbury. In 1982, the noisy, crashing docks that had been at the heart of the City fell silent.

But already in 1981 the spectacular land-and-waterscape of the redundant Docklands was earmarked to become a government-sponsored Enterprise Zone and Europe's largest urban redevelopment project. While the bulldozers moved in to create a dream water-city with the Canary Wharf complex at its heart, the City fathers looked on, then made their move. When exchange controls were abolished at the Big Bang of 1985-6, they held on to as much trade as possible by responding quickly to demands for a new kind of office space that could accommodate modern technology. Over the next eight years, half the City was rebuilt. Thomas Gresham, Founder of the Royal Exchange, would have been proud.

THE MERCHANTS' CITY AND PORT

Despite the City's recurring redevelopment booms, traditional lifestyles and old buildings survive in remarkable quantity. Broadgate was the City's largest development of the 1980s: state-of-the-art offices, restaurants, sculptures and a health-club fill thirteen buildings around three squares. The scheme was inspired by the huge façades and overwhelming lobbies of North American office design. Broadgate Square is the central public area, whose restaurants and terraces surround an amphitheatre that is used as an ice rink in winter. Richard Seera's sculpture, Fulcrum (left), *its vast steel sheets resting against each other, marks one entrance to the square.*

Not far away, tradition rules in Aldgate's Petticoat Lane Market (right), whose Sunday traders spread into neighbouring Middlesex Street. In the seventeenth century, old clothes were sold here in the countryside outside the City walls. By the mid-eighteenth century the area was a trading centre, and by Victorian times the Sunday market was the largest in London for second-hand goods. Today, shops and stalls trade all day on Sunday, selling new and old goods of all kinds. The market spreads into the surrounding streets, and traders humour their customers with Cockney jokes and rhyming slang.

Down by the Thames, the view from Southwark Bridge (overleaf) encompasses both old and new. The domes of Cannon Street Station's two triumphal towers, built in 1865-6, are silhouetted against the night sky, while the floodlit shaft and pyramid roof of Canary Wharf Tower, completed in 1991, are equally dramatic.

THE SEAT OF POWER

THE CITY OF WESTMINSTER, VICTORIA, WHITEHALL AND TRAFALGAR SQUARE

'They thought that Mr Disraeli would produce an extraordinary sensation by the power and splendour of his eloquence. But . . . He was assailed by groans and under-growls in all their varieties; the uproar, indeed, often became so great as completely to drown his voice. At last, losing all temper, he paused in the midst of a sentence, raised his hands, and opening his mouth as wide as its dimensions would permit, said, in remarkably loud and almost terrific tones, "Though I sit down now, the time will come when you will hear me!" '

This anonymous account of Benjamin Disraeli's disastrous maiden speech in 1837 captures the theatre and the open democratic debate that are the essence of Westminster. Even today, visitors to the House of Commons witness ferocious public cross-questioning.

The City of Westminster, unlike the secretive City of London which operates behind the closed doors of its grand façades, lives its life in public, using some of London's grandest buildings as a backdrop. Its three powerhouses – Westminster Abbey, the Houses of Parliament and Buckingham Palace – are all central to that public life and reinforce Westminster's position as the temporal and spiritual headquarters of the sovereign, who is head of church and state, and of the Commonwealth, and of her government.

Westminster was founded on religion. On the boggy banks of the Tyburn river, more than 2 miles (3 km) upstream from the busy, walled City of London, the church of St Peter was established in 604, possibly by Sebert, king of the East Saxons. Subsequent kings and worthies endowed St Peter's. Edgar gave land, Canute relics, then, around 960, St Dunstan, Bishop of London, provided a dozen Benedictine monks to start a monastery.

But the real creator of Westminster was Edward the Confessor. Dreaming of a new palace, a monastery and an abbey church fit for royal burial, his religious fervour was redoubled when Pope Leo allowed him to restore Westminster's monastery instead of making a pilgrimage to Rome. Edward began his new Romanesque church, and in about 1060 left Wardrobe Palace in the City for the Palace of Westminster.

From then on, rulers at Westminster and merchants in the City would enjoy a distant but tense relationship. The former constantly

needed money for wars, crusades or extravagant lifestyles; the latter could supply that money but would do so only in return for power.

Edward's abbey was consecrated on 28 December 1065. Eight days later he died, but his dream continued without him, propelled by the need to fuse religion and state. When William the Conqueror was crowned with great ritual in the abbey on Christmas Day 1066, he began a tradition which was as much political as spiritual. It was in that tradition that Elizabeth II was crowned in 1953. Nine processions of 250 people escorted her to the abbey and during the four-hour ceremony she sat on three chairs and wore four sets of clothes. She was crowned with St Edward's Crown, but left the abbey wearing the Imperial State Crown.

Successive kings lavished money on the abbey. Henry III began by adding the Lady Chapel then, in 1245, employed Henry de Reyns to start rebuilding it all in the new, soaring Gothic style, with the intention of making it into a combination of shrine to Edward the Confessor, grand coronation church and royal necropolis. Richard II, Henry V, Henry VII and donations from pilgrims to the shrine further funded the abbey to near-completion.

Then, in 1532, Henry VIII broke with Rome. The following year the King took the wealthy Benedictine monastery as Crown property. Deprived of its monks, the abbey became the shrine, coronation church and royal burial site Henry III had dreamed of. The royal tombs and the Confessor's Chapel lie at its heart, amidst monuments to politicians, scientists, poets and philanthropists. Until the late nineteenth century, burial rights at the abbey could be bought, so not all those interred here are especially virtuous.

The crowd of grandly entombed sovereigns begins with Edward the Confessor – although one tomb may even be that of the founder Sebert – and ends with George II, after whose death Windsor Castle became the royal family's preferred place of burial.

For visitors today, the abbey's cloisters are an evocative reminder of its past. Outside the abbey's great west door, more old monastic buildings are occupied by Westminster School, whose former pupils include Ben Jonson and Sir Christopher Wren.

The Palace of Westminster, better known as the Houses of Parliament, is the pulse of Westminster. Seen from the south end of Westminster Bridge (previous page), or from across the lake in St James's Park (left), it sets the tone for London's second city.

'It is observable, that our kings and queens make always two solemn visits to this church, and very rarely, if ever, come here any more, viz. To be crown'd and to be buried ... It is become such a piece of honour to be buried in Westminster-Abbey, that the body of the church begins to be crowded with the bodies of citizens, poets, seamen and parsons, nay even with very mean persons, if they have but any way made themselves known in the world; so that in time, the royal ashes will be thus mingled with common dust, that it will leave no room either for king or common people, or at least not for their monuments, some of which also are rather pompously foolish, than solid and to the purpose.'

Daniel Defoe, *A Tour Thro' the Whole Island of Great Britain*, 1724-7

THE SEAT OF POWER

WESTMINSTER ABBEY
When Defoe was writing his account of London in the 1720s, he noted that Westminster Abbey was 'a venerable old pile of a building' that was in the process of having 'great cost bestowed in upholding and repairing it'. Nicholas Hawksmoor was the architect who, as his last public work, restored the abbey and added the West Towers (left) in 1735-45. By this time, Edward the Confessor's church had been replaced twice – first by a Norman church, then by an ambitious Gothic building begun by Henry III in 1245; the nave was completed in the 1390s. Despite Hawksmoor's efforts to respect the Gothic style, the flat corner buttresses and broad string-courses reveal his English Baroque hand. The sculpture of St George slaying the dragon (right) tops the appropriately Gothic monument designed by George Gilbert Scott to commemorate pupils of the adjacent Westminster School who died in the Crimean War.

Edward the Confessor's Palace of Westminster is today better known as the Houses of Parliament. William the Conqueror, having captured a London 'overflowing' with people and 'richer in treasure than the rest of the kingdom', decided to move the royal court there from Winchester, and chose the Palace of Westminster as his London residence. His son William II's addition to the palace – Westminster Hall, later rebuilt by Richard II – was where the foundations of modern Parliament were laid. Here, in 1295, attended by elected knights, citizens and burgesses, Edward I presided over the Model Parliament, while the lower clergy sat with the lords to advise the king. Thus, the principles of England's government were established. Soon after Edward's death, the elected Commons began to meet separately, in Westminster Abbey's Chapter House among other places, while the Lords met in the king's presence in the Painted Chamber at the Palace of Westminster.

When royal chapels were secularized after Henry VIII's Reformation, the Commons moved into Westminster Palace's small, two-storeyed St Stephen's Chapel, completed by Edward III and exquisitely decorated with sculptures, stained glass and wall paintings. It was here that, from the time of Edward VI to William IV – that is, from 1527 until a disastrous fire in 1834 – all the great events in English parliamentary history were played out.

In the early seventeenth century the struggle for constitutional government took place here. In January 1642, Charles I burst in to demand the arrest of five Members of Parliament. He was refused, since when no sovereign has been allowed to enter the Commons' chamber. In the eighteenth century, Edmund Burke pleaded for an understanding of the American colonies, William Pitt the Elder and Henry Fox debated

peace and war in Europe during the War of Austrian Succession, and later that century and early in the next, William Wilberforce argued for the abolition of slavery.

In 1834, fire destroyed the Palace of Westminster. Only Westminster Hall, the cloisters and the Jewel Tower survived. Charles Barry and Augustus Welby Pugin won the competition to design a new building. Today's House of Commons echoes its predecessor, with MPs facing each other in parallel rows like a choir in a chapel. Here, in this newer room, Winston Churchill gave his calls to arms during the Second World War, Clement Attlee pleaded for a welfare state and Margaret Thatcher, Britain's first woman prime minister, forced through her aggressive monetary policy.

With its size, spires and sculptures, the new Palace of Westminster usurped the abbey's position as Westminster's prime landmark. Seen from the river, its long façade of clock tower (Big Ben), House of Commons, Lobby, House of Lords and Victoria Tower combine to look more like a fairytale castle than a forum for political debate.

The surroundings of the Houses of Parliament are suffused with politics too. A posse of prime ministers' statues overlooks Parliament Square, amongst them Robert Peel, Benjamin Disraeli, Viscount Palmerston and Sir Winston Churchill. On the south side of the square stands St Margaret's Church, where MPs have worshipped ever since the Puritans forsook the richness of the abbey in 1614. On the west side, behind the decorative Middlesex Guildhall, rises the domed Methodist Central Hall, where the first assembly of the United Nations met in 1948, while on the remaining side stands the ponderously grand Foreign Office, built in the days of Empire and marking the entry to the great sweep of Whitehall.

The original site of the Coade stone lion (left), now standing at the south end of Westminster Bridge, was the Old Lion Brewery near Waterloo station. The lion was made by W.F.W. Coade in 1837, three years before his factory closed and the secret recipe for the compound Coade stone – the most weatherproof artificial stone ever made – was lost.

At the north end of Westminster Bridge stands the Clock Tower of the Houses of Parliament, better known by the name of its bell, Big Ben (right). Charles Barry's plan was for a 316-feet (96-m) tower containing the world's biggest and best clock, designed by the Royal Astronomer, Benjamin Vulliamy. E.J. Dent made the clock. The bell, cast at Stockton-on-Tees in Northumberland, cracked because the clapper was too heavy, so a new bell was cast at Whitechapel, East London. The 14-feet- (4-m-) long minute hands, originally of cast iron, were too heavy to work properly, so they were recast in gunmetal, then in hollow copper. They finally went into action on 31 May 1859.

THE CATHOLIC CATHEDRAL

Views from the balconies of Westminster Cathedral's Campanile – 273 feet (83 m) up and one of the few public aerial views in Westminster – look across the area of Victoria to Westminster Abbey, St Margaret's Church and the Queen's Tower of the Houses of Parliament (left, above), and over the gilded Queen Victoria Memorial and St James's Park to London's West End (left, below).

Victoria grew up over lands belonging to Westminster Abbey. The congested medieval town once famous for its criminals was cleared during the nineteenth century. Victoria Street, built in 1851, is unremarkable except for the neo-Byzantine bulk of Westminster Cathedral (right). After the Roman Catholic hierarchy was re-established in England and Wales in 1850, three centuries after the Reformation, Westminster became the chief see. In 1894 Archbishop Herbert Vaughan appointed Catholic convert John Francis Bentley to design a new cathedral. The building was completed in 1903. The Campanile is dedicated to Edward the Confessor, who, ironically, lies buried in the Protestant Westminster Abbey near by. The interior decoration has some of Bentley's original ideas, including sparkling mosaics in the domes. There are also sculptures by Eric Gill and Elizabeth Frink.

Looking up Whitehall, past the equestrian statue of the Duke of Cambridge towards Nelson's Column in Trafalgar Square (left), it is hard to imagine that this whole area was once covered by the sprawling Tudor timber buildings of Whitehall Palace. Begun by Cardinal Wolsey, it was greatly enlarged when Henry VIII acquired it after Wolsey's disgrace and left Westminster Palace to make it his principal London home.

When Cardinal Wolsey fell from favour in 1529, Henry VIII acquired not only the cardinal's country house, Hampton Court Palace, but also his town mansion, the Palace of Whitehall. This was so impressive that Henry moved into it, adding a complete royal entertainment centre – four tennis courts, a cock-pit, and a tiltyard for tournaments and bear-baiting. Whitehall was to remain the monarch's principal London home until 1689, when William and Mary moved away from the dank riverside to Kensington Palace.

Throughout the seventeenth century, the Stuart kings lived at Whitehall in astonishing splendour. James I dreamed of rebuilding the 2,000-room palace but completed only the Banqueting House. Designed by Inigo Jones in 1619-22 this was London's first building to be faced in Portland stone, and was later decorated by Sir Peter Paul Rubens. Charles I amassed a spectacular art collection at Whitehall, part of which survives in the Queen's Royal Collection and is occasionally displayed at the Queen's Gallery.

Only the Banqueting House survived the fire that rampaged through the Palace of Whitehall in 1698. It was here that Charles I was beheaded on 30 January 1649, ushering in the Commonwealth under Oliver Cromwell; and it was here too that Charles II celebrated his restoration to the throne eleven years later.

Today ministerial buildings housing a labyrinth of civil servants' offices line both sides of the wide street of Whitehall. One small road leading off it is Downing Street where, in 1735, George II gave the house at No. 10 to Robert Peel to be used as the prime minister's official residence. It has remained so ever since, and pictures of the famous front door are flashed around the world by television cameras whenever some newsworthy event involves the British prime minister.

Towards the north end of Whitehall, the seahorses and dolphins of the screen of Admiralty House give a hint of what is to come – Trafalgar Square, laid out over the royal stables to honour Britain's sailor-hero, Horatio, Viscount Nelson. From his high column, Nelson looks down over the statues of lesser heroes, Edwin Lutyens's fountains and the visitors who love to feed the thousands of London pigeons here. The portico of the National Gallery, together with the gallery's modern Sainsbury Wing, opened in 1991, is Nelson's backdrop, while in the nearby National Portrait Gallery a portrait of Nelson's mistress, Lady Hamilton, hangs among Britain's sovereigns and heroes.

A SQUARE FOR ADMIRAL NELSON

Trafalgar Square (left) was laid out in 1830. Until then, it was part meeting place, where Dr Johnson would stand and see 'the full tide of human existence', part mews for the royal hawks, and later royal stables. The plan, originally part of John Nash's extension to his great Regent Street sweep, was made reality by Charles Barry, architect of the Houses of Parliament. The square's three sides are formed by Sir Robert Smirke's Canada House (1824-7), Sir Herbert Baker's South Africa House (1935) and William Wilkins's National Gallery (1832-8).

The square honours Horatio, Viscount Nelson, who was an admiral at the age of thirty-nine and whose naval triumphs included the Battle of St Vincent and the Battle of the Nile. His statue and 185-feet- (56-m-) high column were erected in 1843, with Edwin Landseer's gentle lions added at the base in 1868. Bronze busts of lesser naval commanders stand in the north wall of the square, while the Indian army heroes General Sir Charles James Napier and Sir Henry Havelock flank Nelson's column. Two equestrian statues of sovereigns are also here – Hubert Le Sueur's fine Charles I, made in 1633 and erected by Charles II in 1675; and Francis Chantrey's George IV, placed here in 1843. The elegant fountains and pools (below), with sculptures by Charles Marshall, were Edwin Lutyens's last London works, completed in 1939.

But not even Nelson can compete with the royals as a tourist attraction. Buckingham Palace, together with St James's Palace, is the third of Westminster's powerhouses, and the venue for some of London's finest public displays.

St James's Palace, built by Henry VIII and the seat of the royal court under Elizabeth I and James I, is where Queen Anne and the early Hanoverians lived when not at Kensington Palace or at Hampton Court. Even today, St James's Palace, which is not open to the public, remains the official London residence of the monarch, a fact that is symbolized by the accreditation of foreign ambassadors to the Court of St James's.

Buckingham Palace is a more recent addition. The young George III bought Buckingham House for Queen Charlotte in 1762, making this yet another in the string of royal London homes. Some of its 600 rooms, extravagantly rebuilt by George IV, are open to the public during certain months. They include the State Rooms, the Queen's Gallery and the Royal Mews, where the magnificent apparel of royal ceremony is kept, including the Gold State Coach. Made for George III in 1762 and designed by Sir William Chambers, this coach makes its appearance on the occasion of a coronation, when it carries the sovereign down the Mall and on to Westminster Abbey.

The Mall – built to commemorate Queen Victoria – was created by slicing through St James's Park. At its west end stands Buckingham Palace with its Aston Webb façade, erected in just three months for George V's coronation in 1910; at its east end stands Admiralty Arch. Along the north side, behind an earlier Mall where fashionable London paraded in the eighteenth century, stand Clarence House and Marlborough House, the latter built by Queen Anne's closest friend, the Duchess of Marlborough.

The Mall is the setting for royal pageantry at its best. As well as being decorated for coronations, royal weddings and funerals, on the occasion of a state visit by a foreign leader it is bedecked with Union Jack flags alternating with flags from the country of the visiting dignitary.

For more modest pageantry, there are almost daily displays of the Changing of the Guard at the three palaces – St James's Palace, Buckingham Palace and Whitehall (represented by Horse Guards). The Changing of the Guard has been performed by the Household Division ever since the Restoration of Charles II in 1660. Today it symbolizes the protection of the sovereign by the Army.

An allegory of Victory clothed in gold leaf tops the lavish, white marble Victoria Memorial (above), created by Thomas Brock in 1911. It stands in front of Aston Webb's Buckingham Palace façade, which is guarded by elaborate gates decorated with the gilded royal coat of arms (opposite). The Queen-Empress sits looking along the Mall, the wide, straight road created by Webb to reinforce royal power by enabling British subjects to witness the full panoply of state processions. Much of this ceremonial continues today. On the sovereign's official birthday, for instance, the Queen plays the roles of both sovereign and Commander-in-Chief of the seven regiments of the Household Guards. She goes down the Mall by carriage to Horse Guards, where her birthday is celebrated during the Trooping the Colour ceremony. She then returns to Buckingham Palace to watch a Royal Air Force fly-past from the balcony.

'I went to St. James's Parke, where I examin'd the Throate of the Onocratylus or Pelecan . . . a Melancholy water foule brought from Astracan by the Russian Ambassador . . . The Parke was at this time stored with infinite flocks of severall sorts of ordinary, and extraordinary Wild foule, breeding about the Decoy, which for being neere so greate a Citty, and among such a concourse of Souldiers, Guards and people, is very diverting: There were also Deer of severall countries, White, spotted like Leopards, Antelope: An Elke, Red deeres, Robucks, Staggs, Guinny Goates: Arabian sheepe, etc.'

John Evelyn, *Diary*, 1665

ST JAMES'S PARK

With its views across the lake to Westminster, St James's Park is the oldest and most obviously royal of London's nine royal parks. Buckingham Palace, St James's Palace and Horse Guards - symbolizing the vanished Whitehall Palace - all overlook it, and past sovereigns have used it as their private back garden. Its 93 acres (38 hectares) contain memories of Charles II's Versailles-inspired improvements - an ornamental canal and gardens stocked with fruit trees, birds and animals. George IV employed John Nash to replace this French formality with softly undulating lawns, twisting paths and billowing shrubberies.

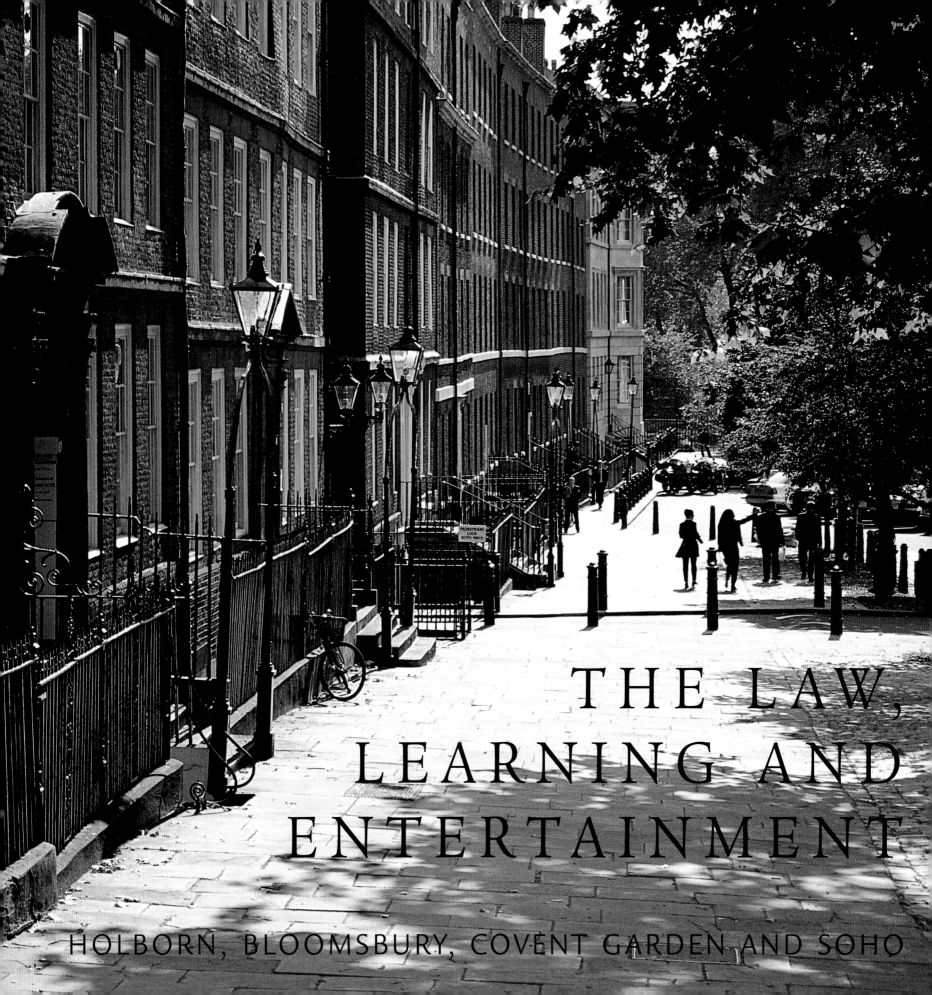

THE LAW, LEARNING AND ENTERTAINMENT

HOLBORN, BLOOMSBURY, COVENT GARDEN AND SOHO

'The lighted shops of Strand and Fleet Street; the innumerable trades, tradesmen and customers, coaches, waggons, playhouses; all the bustle and wickedness round about Covent Garden; the very women of the town; the watchmen, drunken scenes, rattles; lies awake, if you awake, at all hours of the night; the impossibility of being dull in Fleet Street; the crowds, the very dirt and mud, the sun shining upon houses and pavements, the pint-shops, the old bookstalls, parsons cheapening books, coffee houses, steams of soups from kitchens, the pantomime – London itself is a pantomime and masquerade – all these things work themselves into my mind and feed me, without a power of satiating me.'

For Charles Lamb, writing to William Wordsworth in 1801, the focus of London was the streets that stretch from Westminster northwards across Soho, then eastwards across Covent Garden and Bloomsbury, Fleet Street and Holborn. As both the City of London and the City of Westminster grew, often in tense competition, this dynamic area was the common ground between them. The resources both cities needed most were news, education, law and entertainment. Here all were provided in good measure and, with the exception of the news, still are.

Today, for relaxation in this part of town, Londoners can drop into a museum, a café or a theatre, or sit in one of the area's tree-shaded oases. There are the Embankment Gardens, laid over Bazalgette's reclaimed land; those behind the Strand play host to summertime poetry-readings and music. There are the Bloomsbury squares where

university students and visitors to the British Museum take time off. Or there are the gardens of the Inns of Court or Temple. In 1763, Boswell would stroll about the Temple to 'quit the hurry and bustle of the City in Fleet Street and the Strand . . . all at once you find yourself in a pleasant academic retreat. You see good convenient buildings, handsome walks and you view the silver Thames.'

Long before Boswell found such tranquillity, the bridle-path across the fields linking the Cities of London and Westminster attracted bishops, noblemen and courtiers. This path was to become the Strand and Fleet Street. A parade of palaces, often known as inns, rose between the Strand and the river. The Bishop of Salisbury's inn hosted the Spanish envoy in 1554 while he arranged the marriage between Philip II of Spain and Queen Mary. During the Reformation, the inns were redistributed to favoured noblemen. At the beginning of the seventeenth century one nobleman, the Earl of Northumberland, built a vast mansion at the west end of the Strand. His descendants enjoyed it until it was demolished in 1874, having been blocked in by the Embankment on one side and Trafalgar Square on the other, but the name lives on in Northumberland Place.

Eastwards along the Strand stood the mansion of George Villiers, 2nd Duke of Buckingham, whose looks helped propel him from commoner to duke in just seven years. In the 1670s his heirs sold it to one of London's most successful property speculators, Dr Nicholas Barbon. There was one condition – that the mansion's York Watergate be kept. Today it stands at the back of Embankment Gardens, marking the original position of the river bank.

Barbon's buildings, hastily put up, had nevertheless to conform to the regulations devised after the Great Fire of 1666. Walls had to be of brick or stone; a minimum of timber was to be used; front walls were to run up above the roof line to make a parapet, while timber window frames were to be set back from the wall. The simple design that developed from the imposition of these regulations became the hallmark of Georgian London's building boom. The style would be brought to its greatest refinement in the late eighteenth century with the work of the Adam brothers and their followers, for instance in the houses of Robert Street and John Adam Street, survivors of the brothers' Adelphi development.

Whilst most of the once-aristocratic Strand eventually became a knot of shops, theatres and street entertainment overspilling from Covent Garden, Fleet Street's closeness to the City kept it more businesslike. The first book to be printed in England, *Dictes and Sayings of the Philosophers*, came hot off William Caxton's Westminster press

in 1477; and after Caxton's death, his more commercially minded pupil, Wynkyn de Worde, moved the press to Fleet Street to be nearer to his customers – the clergy around St Paul's who had a virtual monopoly on literacy.

Here, near St Bride's Church, de Worde set up England's first printing press with movable type. Between 1500 and his death in 1536, he printed about 800 books. Soon, printers, bookbinders and booksellers filled Fleet Street, spreading into the old bookshop area of St Paul's Churchyard. Coffee-houses and pubs, the meeting places of such people, came too, as did writers. Dr Samuel Johnson moved into Gough Square, off Fleet Street, in 1749. Here, helped by six amanuenses in the top-floor garret, he compiled his famous dictionary, and bravely broke reporting restrictions by writing reports for news-hungry Londoners that were thinly veiled as coming from Swift's imaginary land of Lilliput. Today, Dr Johnson's house is more evocative of the world of writers and printers than anything else in Fleet Street. Sadly, the newspapers that thrived on 'The Street' in the mid-twentieth century – with their hardened journalists, press-baron owners and thundering presses – have all moved away.

What do remain are the Inns of Court, lurking down lanes and behind tall walls. Their beginnings probably lay in the mansions of the clergy, where students and barristers, originally under the control of the clergy, continued to live even after Edward I put them under the judges. In the nineteenth century, the many Inns were rationalized to four, and the courts dotted about London were centralized to make one Royal Court of Justice. Today, this cathedral-like building is the barristers' own public theatre, surrounded by wig-makers, tailors for their gowns and shops selling legal books.

London's legal world has some fine buildings and street furniture. The bricks for King's Bench Walk (previous page) were rubbed to a precise size so the joints could be thinner. Gilded lamps stand in front of the Royal Courts of Justice, G.E. Street's Gothic fantasy (opposite), while the old Daily Telegraph Building's clock (above) lingers on despite the press's exodus from Fleet Street.

LINCOLN'S INN

Today, most visitors to Lincoln's Inn Fields are on their way to see the treasure-filled home and museum (left) of architect and antiquarian Sir John Soane, who died in 1837. But the square's legal importance is also considerable, and has a long history. Lincoln's Inn Fields was built in the 1660s as an ambitious speculation by William Newton and, despite the many London squares built subsequently, remains the largest. Shaded by mature plane trees, it has over the years attracted half a dozen Lords Chancellor. One was Lord Mansfield who, as Chief Justice, declared slavery illegal in 1772. To crown his successful career, he employed Robert Adam to remodel Kenwood House as his summer retreat in Hampstead.

Lord Mansfield had chambers in Inner Temple, one of the four Inns of Court. Inner and Middle Temples lie off Fleet Street, where the network of barristers' chambers and tranquil squares and gardens surrounding a circular twelfth-century church are built on land that once belonged to the Knights Templar. The other two Inns – Gray's and Lincoln's – are in Holborn. Both have their illustrious past members. Gray's Inn has Elizabeth I's Secretary of State, William Cecil, and the 3rd Earl of Southampton who, as Shakespeare's patron, first staged *The Comedy of Errors*, which was performed in the Inn's dining hall. Lincoln's Inn has produced an impressive list of prime ministers – Walpole, Pitt the Younger, Melbourne, Asquith, Disraeli and Gladstone.

Seen through Brewster Gate (right), Lincoln's Inn has a collegiate atmosphere similar to the colleges of Oxford and Cambridge. Buildings surrounding the peaceful lawns include Old Hall, built in the 1490s, the seventeenth-century chapel and the Victorian Library, housing London's oldest collection of books, begun in 1497.

'If anybody still believes that Sir John Soane was a neo-classical architect, let him go to Lincoln's Inn Fields and see what Soane did in the exterior and interior of his own house ... The house is a combination of living quarters, studio, and museum and as such decidedly congested. However, it was just that congestion that set Soane's genius off to create the most unexpected and capricious spatial interplay ... The goal throughout is to confuse and mystify, and what goal could be less classical?'

Nikolaus Pevsner, *The Buildings of England, London, Vol. I*, 1957

Newton's Lincoln's Inn Fields was inspired by Covent Garden, London's first residential square. After the Dissolution of the Monasteries in 1536, the convent garden of Westminster Abbey was given to the 1st Earl of Bedford. In 1631 he employed Inigo Jones, Charles I's favourite architect, to develop it. Taking his inspiration from the Place des Vosges in Paris and the piazzas of Italy, Jones created order and space among London's tight-knit streets. Here, the new houses, set behind their unified Classical and stuccoed façades, looked across the open square to St Paul's Church.

The square was the prototype for much of the capital's development over the next 250 years. It proved a success as a residential area until, in 1671, the 5th Earl of Bedford won a licence to hold a fruit and vegetable market in its centre. High society, already moving westwards to the new developments of St James's and Mayfair after the Great Fire of 1666, moved out.

Covent Garden was left to become an amusement park. Taverns and Turkish baths, theatres and gambling dens, pickpockets and prostitutes soon earned the square its nickname 'the great square of Venus'. By the nineteenth century, so many traders had left the City for this lucrative area that a string of market buildings went up, starting with Charles Fowler's Central Market in 1831. Theatres mushroomed, and such a crush of people and unsavoury entertainment overflowed down on to the Strand that the de luxe Savoy Hotel, opened in 1889, put its main entrance on the Embankment rather than on the Strand.

In the twentieth century, a post-war government plan to bulldoze Covent Garden roused its people to wage a campaign not merely to save the buildings, but to rejuvenate the whole area. They succeeded, and today Covent Garden throbs with life. Craft markets and museums fill the old fruit and flower market buildings. St Paul's Church, always loved by actors, is now the backdrop for street entertainers. And amid all the restaurants and shops, the elitist Royal Opera House has even projected its performances on to huge screens in the Piazza for opera-hungry crowds. Once again, Covent Garden is an amusement park for everyone.

The Earl of Bedford started a fresh produce market in Covent Garden Piazza in 1671. Three centuries later, the market spirit survives in the stalls, shops and restaurants filling Charles Fowler's 1831 building.

Covent Garden's success has rubbed off on its neighbours. To the north lie Bloomsbury's many squares built from the late seventeenth century onwards – simple Bloomsbury Square, large and leafy Russell Square, Tavistock Square and Gordon Square, and the near-perfect Bedford Square were all developed over monastic land and named after the Bedford family's various titles. Now, many of Bloomsbury's buildings house departments of the sprawling University of London.

But Bloomsbury's heart is the British Museum, much reorganized after the British Library's move to its own purpose-built home in Euston Road. This new building extends Bloomsbury's intellectual life northwards to where the Victorians proudly built the stations of St Pancras, King's Cross and Euston to bring trains from the Midlands and the north into their prosperous capital.

The British Museum is now the focus of a museum route that runs southwards from the British Library through Bloomsbury and Covent Garden to the river. Along it are museums of Jewish culture and Chinese porcelain, Covent Garden's museums of theatre and transport and, down at the Aldwych, the Courtauld Institute of Art displaying its Impressionist paintings, silver and other treasures in the palatial riverside Somerset House.

Robert Smirke's Neoclassical British Museum (above), completed in 1847, was all that early Victorians expected of their public cultural buildings. Professor Sir Colin St John Wilson's British Library (right), opened in 1997, presents a striking contrast to the Georgian architecture of Bloomsbury, with its strong horizontals and red bricks.

BEDFORD SQUARE

Bedford Square (right and below) was London's first square to be planned and built as a self-contained architectural unit. It was a developer's daring speculation, probably designed by Thomas Leverton, who lived at No. 1. Work began in the mid-1770s and took about ten years. Today it remains London's most complete and perfect square. Each side is a simple design, a great palace façade with a central pediment. Within this restrained simplicity, there is rich detailing and both exteriors and interiors are of unusually high craftsmanship.

As with many other London squares, Bedford Square was originally gated and guarded, giving residents extra privacy. Carriages were permitted to enter but tradesmen had to use the back doors in the mews lanes behind. The central garden was, and still is, reserved for residents.

Soho's response to Covent Garden's renaissance has been equally dramatic. The area lies to the south-west of Bloomsbury, across St Martin's Lane with its theatres, and Charing Cross Road with its bookshops. At the Dissolution of the Monasteries, Henry VIII kept for himself the tract of land that is now known as Soho, to extend his hunting land from Whitehall Palace. Later he parcelled it out to royal favourites, who used it to build their country houses.

It was Soho's immigrants who gave the area its exotic character. Huguenots arrived first, fleeing religious persecution in France. By the 1740s, French traders dominated the area, by which time the British aristocrats had departed westwards. In the nineteenth and twentieth centuries Italians and Sicilians, fleeing political persecution, created an atmosphere which their descendants keep alive today in their Italian shops, delicatessens and patisseries.

Next, in the 1950s and 1960s, Chinese arrived from Hong Kong and China, fleeing poverty in the New Territories. They set up their own fishmongers, grocers, herbalists and bakeries in Soho's southern streets, and introduced *dim sum* and the pageantry of Chinese New Year to London.

During the nineteenth century, Soho had become a centre for entertainment with theatres, music halls and prostitutes. Today, this element has almost gone. The friendly seediness of the prostitutes, peepshows and striptease clubs that were once an integral part of the area was nearly wiped out after the Westminster Council crackdown began in 1986. Now, quantities of restaurants and bars have replaced them – so many that a summer evening promenade down Dean, Greek or Old Compton Streets is like progressing through one big party. Perhaps the epitome of all this change is Sir Terence Conran's Mezzo, a deafeningly loud, 350-seater, state-of-the-art bar and restaurant on the site of the original Marquee Club.

London's Chinatown celebrates Chinese New Year with a street carnival and the traditional lion dance. On this day, Chinese restaurants and shops are at their busiest, traditional Chinese gambling abounds, red envelopes of 'luck money' are handed out and there are cries of 'Gung Hei Faat Choi' ('Wishing you prosperity'). Activities centre on Gerrard Street, where the local council's gift of Chinese red-and-gold gateways, telephone boxes and benches recognizes the community's strength. Today, about half of Britain's 100,000 Chinese live in Soho, calling their district Tong Yan Kai (Chinese Street).

WEST-END ENTERTAINMENT

Leicester Square (left) is the hub of London's entertainment world. A square like no other in London, it is an incongruous mixture of cinemas, restaurants and amusement halls, all advertising themselves with huge, flashing neon signs, all surrounding a quiet oasis of mature London plane trees. The oasis is a survivor from the days when handsome houses lined the square. In the eighteenth century it was popular with artists – William Hogarth, Sir Joshua Reynolds and the American John Singleton Copley lived here.

The square's character began to change in the nineteenth century. Residents moved out as hotels, shops and other entertainments moved in – the Alhambra Theatre opened in 1858. By the turn of the century its dives, clubs and restaurants were enjoyed mainly by men: it was no place for a lady to go unescorted.

The arrival of the picture palaces introduced London to the glamour of American culture, and this new mass entertainment demanded a clean-up. The Empire cinema opened in 1928, the Odeon in 1937 and the Warner West End the following year. High society patronized its clubs where stars such as Marlene Dietrich and Noël Coward sang through the night.

Today, the spirit of entertainment continues. Glittering film premières are held here. Statues of Charlie Chaplin and William Shakespeare, two great entertainers, stand in the square, while near by, at Piccadilly Circus, Madame Tussaud's *Rock Circus* overlooks one of London's best-known statues, Alfred Gilbert's *Angel of Christian Charity*, better known as *Eros*. From here, theatre-lined Shaftesbury Avenue sweeps up to Cambridge Circus, while across Tottenham Court Road, past more theatres and through dark alleys, the Coliseum in St Martin's Lane (right), built in 1904, is the grand Edwardian home of the English National Opera.

'Closed in the summer of 1940, [the Café de Paris in Leicester Square] had reopened three months later at the height of the Blitz, and was still the smartest place for young officers on leave to take their girls . . . amid the infectious rhythm, the popping of champagne corks and the happy buzz of conversation, you could not hear the noise of the raids . . . There was a curious pinging sound – one dancer thought it was the signal for a novelty number – and a blue flash, and then everything blew up. Two fifty-kilo bombs had fallen down an air shaft through the Rialto and directly on to the dance floor of the Café de Paris.'

Carol Kennedy, *Mayfair, A Social History*, 1986

ARTS AND ARISTOCRATS

ST JAMES'S AND MAYFAIR

When it was first completed, Constitution Arch (previous page), designed by Decimus Burton in 1827-9, stood nearer to Apsley House, marking the west entrance to London. Moved to its present position in 1883, it is now the focus for one of Europe's busiest roundabouts. Constitution Arch originally led into Piccadilly and the grand eighteenth-century mansions of Mayfair and St James's. But its public grandeur contrasts sharply with the area's older buildings and alleys. At the southern end of St James's Street, Berry Bros. & Rudd Ltd (above) at No. 3 has a fine panelled interior and a maze of underground cellars where a stock of fine wines is kept. This shop and its neighbour, James Lock & Co. Ltd, Hatters, were once owned by William Pickering. He traded here from 1703, and on the profits, built the houses of Pickering Place (right) next door in 1730.

'Last night, party at Lansdowne House. Tonight, party at Lady Charlotte Greville's – deplorable waste of time, and something of temper. Nothing imparted – nothing acquired – talking without ideas ... Heigho! I have also been drinking, and, on one occasion, with three other friends at the Cocoa Tree, from six till four, yea, until five in the matin. We clareted and champagned till two – then supped, and finished with a king of regency punch composed of madeira, brandy, and green tea, no real water being admitted therein. There was a night for you!'

After his *Childe Harold's Pilgrimage* was published in 1812 and made him an overnight literary sensation, Lord Byron, who wrote this entry in his journal in 1814, lived for a spell on Piccadilly. His home was in London's first and most exclusive apartment house, the Albany. Here he alternated rigorous ascetic regimes with bouts of high living, enjoying the best that the aristocratic mansions and clubs of Mayfair and St James's could offer.

A century later, life was little different. When Walter H. Page arrived in Grosvenor Square in 1913 as the American Ambassador, he was prepared for a burnt-out civilization peopled by the effete and decadent. What he found were men 'gently bred, high-minded, physically fit'. He greatly admired the English for 'their art of high living ... when they make their money they stop money-making and cultivate their minds and their gardens and entertain their friends and do all the high arts of living – to perfection ... I guess they really believe that the earth belongs to them.'

The gracious living of St James's and Mayfair – which had existed since the area was developed – was an increasing anomaly amid the industrial and social change of the twentieth century, especially after the First World War. Yet in the 1920s, Berkeley Street was still lined with the extensive gardens of Devonshire House and Lansdowne House that ran all the way from Piccadilly to Berkeley Square. Even after the Second World War and further profound social changes such as the introduction of inheritance tax, grand mansions still formed a solid stretch from Regent Street to Park Lane. In the end, however, it was the aristocrats' blind apathy rather than bombs in the City or heavy taxes that laid this Central London goldmine open to post-war developers seeking sites for offices and hotels.

The area of St James's and Mayfair is unusual in London for the unity of tone in its building, its lifestyle and in the way it is closely involved with the arts. These three characteristics have lasted from the time it was developed until today.

The building was carried out in bursts. After the Restoration of Charles II in 1660 and the Great Fire of London in 1666, the wealthy merchants and aristocrats of the crowded City began to move west, beyond the City, Covent Garden and the Strand in search of space, safety and healthy air. The attraction was originally the Court at Westminster. Then, when St James's Palace became the official royal residence after the Whitehall Palace fire of 1698, the fate of the fields sloping up behind the palace was sealed.

In 1665, Charles II had been persuaded by his friend Henry Jermyn, Earl of St Albans, to part with some land. Soon St James's Square was laid out and plots of land on the wide streets surrounding it were leased to speculative builders. The redevelopment was enclosed by Jermyn Street, the Haymarket, Pall Mall and St James's Street. It was an instant success. The wealthy moved in to the fashionable addresses in their droves, with servants indoors and coachmen in the mews. Suppliers followed, many of whom still thrive today, some holding royal warrants. James Lock & Co. Ltd, the hatters in St James's Street, is one such and proudly displays royal coats of arms above the shop door. To make way for the building, the Haymarket's twice-weekly fair for cattle and sheep was moved to Mayfair and by 1720, two fashionable theatres were opened, Her Majesty's and the Theatre Royal, where a play's first night is still an occasion for dressing-up.

By now the Hanoverians had been on the throne for six years. Their court language and many of their courtiers were German. George I was homesick and unpopular but his reputation was saved by his passion for music, a passion which inspired him to bring the German composer George Frideric Handel to London. George I's son George II fared little better in the popularity stakes, but his grandson, George III, king from 1760 until 1820, did endear himself to the British people. Meanwhile, Georgian London expanded as never before.

Piccadilly, an old route leading out of London, was soon lined with mansions, each generation building with increased grandeur. When Lord and Lady Melbourne rebuilt their Melbourne House in 1774, they employed Sir William Chambers to design the building, James Paine to design the chimneypieces, Thomas Chippendale to furnish it, and Giovanni Cipriani from Italy to paint the ceiling of the 52-feet- (16-m-) long salon. Having lavished £100,000 on the house, the Melbournes lived a glittering social life, with Elizabeth Melbourne enjoying several affairs – then almost a social requirement – including one with Prince George, the future Prince Regent. By 1802, with Henry Holland's extensions, the mansion had become the Albany, the exclusive apartments where Lord Byron, Thomas Macaulay and Robert Smirke and more recently Sir Edward Heath would all live, and where Jane Austen's brother would run a bank in the courtyard.

West of here lay Green Park, a carefully planted royal playground where today's Londoners stroll among the daffodils and bask in

Spencer House (above), designed by John Vardy for Earl Spencer in the 1750s, has two façades – one on St James's Place, and this one overlooking leafy Green Park.

deckchairs. In Georgian times, entertainment consisted of duels, ballooning and firework displays. In 1748, Handel's specially written music accompanied a firework display in the park, celebrating the end of the War of the Austrian Succession.

By now, inspired by the success of Henry Jermyn's development, builders were testing the fields north of Piccadilly as sites for development. By the mid-eighteenth century, almost all of Mayfair was covered with houses, most of them on seven estates – the Burlington, Millfield, Conduit, Albemarle, Berkeley, Curzon and, by far the largest, the Grosvenor.

The Earl of Scarborough got in early. By 1714, he had built the first of Mayfair's three great squares, Hanover Square, at the centre of the Millfield estate. Soon after, Nathaniel Curzon began laying out his estate, which included the unequivocally aristocratic Curzon Street. Edward Shepherd's little knot of lanes beside it, Shepherd Market, followed. Near by, the Berkeley Estate was a grand, spacious development focused on Mayfair's second great square, Berkeley Square. Here, William Kent's exquisite No. 44, built in the 1740s, is now home to two clubs – the Clermont and Annabel's.

Meanwhile, Henry Jermyn's business consortium that had snapped up the Albemarle estate early in 1683 had suffered financial disaster. However, the streets that were built almost immediately became a shopping success, focused on Bond Street – the eighteenth-century *beau monde* that frequented them being dubbed the 'Bond Street Loungers'. Their conspicuous consumption is imitated by today's big spenders, who buy jewellery

from Boucheron, art from Sotheby's or trinkets from Asprey's.

But all this was small fry. Mayfair's greatest developer was the Grosvenor family. In 1677, the twenty-one-year-old Sir Thomas Grosvenor from Eaton, Cheshire, made an excellent marriage. His bride, twelve-year-old Mary Davies, was set to inherit 100 acres (40 hectares) in Mayfair and another 400 acres (160 hectares) south of Hyde Park. The Mayfair land was developed in 1720-40 and the rest from the 1820s on to form Belgravia and Pimlico. Today, 300 acres (120 hectares) of London are still controlled by the Grosvenors, including some of London's most prestigious addresses in Mayfair and Belgravia.

It was Sir Thomas's son, Richard, who developed Mayfair on a grand scale. Grosvenor Square, Mayfair's third great square, was its centrepiece, surrounded by wide streets of fashionable, yet rather plain, flat-fronted, brick houses, with mews lanes for carriages and horses behind. In an area replete with aristocrats, none drew more dukes, marquises, earls and viscounts than Grosvenor Square. Later, London's most discerning de luxe hotel, the Connaught, would open near by. Claridge's, down the road in Brook Street, was rebuilt in 1895-9 by Richard D'Oyly Carte using the profits from his operetta *The Mikado*. Today, royal guests on state visits to London stay here after their few days at Buckingham Palace. From Mayfair, the rich and landed spilled over Oxford Street on to the Marylebone and Portman estates, then into Bayswater overlooking Hyde Park. But St James's and Mayfair remained the 'focus for feudal grandeur, fashion, taste and hospitality', and in many ways are so today.

The size of Grosvenor Square (above), built 1725-53, demanded buildings of a similarly imposing scale, although the contemporary critic James Ralph deemed them 'little better than a collection of whims'.

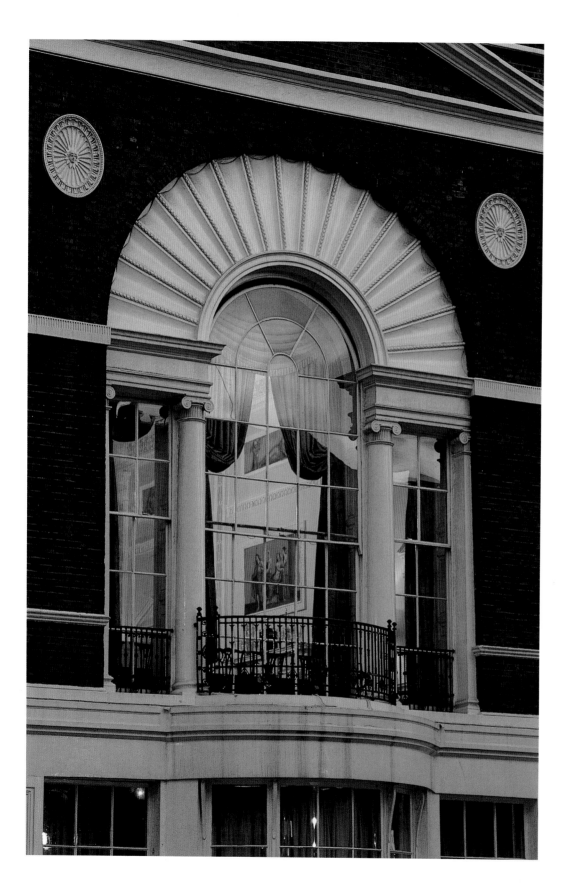

'At White's we see nothing but what wears the Mask of Gaiety and Pleasure. Powder and Embroidery are the Ornaments of the Place, not to forget that intolerable Stink of Perfumes which almost poysons the miserable Chair-men that besiege the Door. Conversation is not known here. The enquiries after the News turn chiefly upon what happen'd last Night at the Groom-Porter's.'

The London Journal, 1727

Of all the St James's coffee-houses which developed into gentlemen's clubs, White's (right), housed in James Wyatt's 1787-8 building behind Lockyer's façade of 1852, is the oldest and the most exclusive. Opened in 1693, it served Turkish coffee – 'that bitter black drincke for quickening their wits' – as well as beer and spirits. It also encouraged gambling, soon the most profitable part of its business. It became so fashionable that its regulars forced the owner to make it a private club. Privileged members have included George IV, Edward VII and every prime minister from Robert Walpole to Robert Peel.
Boodle's Club (left) attracted quite a different crowd. Standing on White's original site, the 1775 clubhouse by John Crunden has a distinctive central Venetian window. Always more of a country gentlemen's club – smart, social and non-political – its reputation nevertheless rested on gambling and good food.

In eighteenth-century St James's and Mayfair, all the necessary facilities were on hand for a lifestyle of pleasure. Gambling was a favourite pastime – Byron and Beau Brummell lost handsomely at the high-stake games of macao and whist. Today's gamblers lose just as impressively in Robert Adam's Crockford's Club in Curzon Street.

In the nineteenth century more sombre club life evolved on Pall Mall, where several clubs were founded to give a gentleman privacy for debating, reading, eating or simply sleeping. (Only now are these clubs beginning to welcome lady members.) Each club had its own character, to some extent preserved today. The Reform Club's magnificent clubhouse, designed by Charles Barry as an Italianate palazzo, was where nineteenth-century Whigs such as Gladstone, Palmerston and Asquith gathered. The Athenaeum attracted an intellectual membership which included academics, government ministers and bishops, while the Travellers' Club still requires prospective members to submit details of their travel adventures.

*'Quite a new order of things has come up:
from small social meetings held periodically, the
clubs have become permanent establishments,
luxurious in all their appointments – some of them
indeed occupy buildings which are quite palatial . . .
they could count their numbers by hundreds and,
sleeping accommodation excepted, provide for them
abundantly all the comforts and luxuries of an
aristocratic home and admirably regulated ménage,
without any of the trouble inseparable from a
private household. Each member of a club is
expected to leave his private address with the
secretary; but this, of course, remains unknown to
the outside world, and considerable advantage
frequently results from the arrangement . . .'*

Edward Walford, *London Recollected,* 1872-8

ST JAMES'S CLUBS

While White's and Boodle's clubs were famous for
their gambling throughout the eighteenth century,
The Athenaeum (right) redressed the balance. This St
James's club was founded in 1824 by John Wilson Croker,
a politician and writer who first coined the term
'Conservative'. It drew and still draws its membership from
the intellectual establishment. Members have included
most prime ministers, major literary figures and an
abundance of bishops.

Called simply 'The Society' at first, following the
move into Decimus Burton's distinguished classical
revival clubhouse on Pall Mall in 1830 it was renamed
'The Athenaeum' after the Athenian temple that served as
a meeting place for the learned. The façade was decorated,
at Croker's insistence, with John Henning's reconstruction
of a frieze on the Parthenon, and with E.H. Baily's great
statue of Athene, Goddess of Wisdom, Industry and War.

For the rich, shopping was a pleasure bordering on addiction. Select shops, founded to serve the courtiers of St James's, thrived. In 1730, Juan Famenias Floris, a perfumer from Minorca, began selling perfumes to the aristocrats, while a Suffolk cheesemonger came to London a decade later and opened Paxton and Whitfield. Both are still in business today.

Jermyn Street's shirtmakers arrived in the nineteenth century, as did Savile Row's tailors; both streets are still centres of pilgrimage for men seeking traditional English tailoring. On Piccadilly, William Fortnum, a footman in Queen Anne's rambling household, opened a grocer's in 1707, now Fortnum and Mason's. Hatchards bookshop opened in 1797, and became more of a club than a shop for bibliophiles such as Gladstone and Macaulay. Bond Street was simply the ultimate de luxe shopping thoroughfare.

Then, in 1909, Gordon Selfridge opened his all-American department store amid Oxford Street's throng of little shops. He introduced a new style of shopping which revolutionized the English retail business. Today, 2-mile- (3-km-) long Oxford Street is the retail capital of Britain.

Art was another of the pleasures of the rich. Paintings, sculptures and other *objets d'art* were constantly needed to furnish new homes and impress visitors. Christie's, the auctioneers, were on hand in King Street to clear the houses of people whose pleasures had landed them in debt, and to provide the newly wealthy with stylish furnishings they might wish they had inherited. Christie's stock was also enriched by a flow of art into London from France where the Revolution was taking its toll of French aristocrats.

Collectors who benefited included the discerning Hertford family, whose Wallace Collection gathered by four generations is now housed in their Manchester Square mansion. The Royal Academy, founded in 1768 with George III as patron and Joshua Reynolds as President, had always been an arbiter of contemporary taste. In 1837 it moved into Lord Burlington's distinguished house on Piccadilly, designed by Colen Campbell in 1715-17. Gradually, the area attracted more and more art dealers, making it the centre of the world art trade that it still is today.

As well as money, essential qualities in an eighteenth-century hostess were taste, a sharp wit, strong political allegiance and beauty. Georgiana, wife of the 5th Duke of Devonshire, had them all. Arriving in London in 1774, aged eighteen, she made Devonshire House on

ARTS AND ARISTOCRATS

Piccadilly a glittering centre of Whig opposition to George III's duller Tory court. Sheridan, Gibbon, Johnson, Charles James Fox and others joined her privileged circle of the brightest and most sophisticated English minds ever to enliven London's balls, card parties, masquerades and routs.

The parties were continuing a century later. In 1873, when the young banker Adrian Hope built Ancaster House off Curzon Street for his four daughters and eighteen servants, he equipped it with the largest private ballroom in London. Even as late as 1925, Lord and Lady Mountbatten, living in the six-storey Brook House, ate off silver plate and were waited on by liveried footmen. And in the run up to their marriage they 'had tea with Mrs Vanderbilt, back in London for the season, dined and danced at the Devonshires, the Blandfords, Lady Carnarvon's and the house of the Chilean Minister. There was also Princess Mary's costume ball for the London Hospitals.'

But the bulldozers eventually arrived and destroyed much of this way of life. Many grand mansions fell like a pack of cards. Dorchester House, modelled on Rome's Villa Farnese, was demolished in the late 1920s to make way for the Art Deco Dorchester Hotel. Some mansions, conveniently close to St James's Palace, were saved by being converted into lavish embassies. These and other survivors give some idea of the opulence and grandeur that had permeated every corner of the area – Apsley House at Hyde Park Corner, with de luxe hotels for neighbours; Spencer House, overlooking Green Park and now painstakingly restored; Crewe House in Curzon Street, still surrounded by its lush gardens; even Byron's Albany apartments.

The English hostesses of the eighteenth and nineteenth centuries in their private palaces have now been replaced by international hostesses who operate from apartments in London, New York, Paris or Palm Beach. When in London they may lunch at the Ritz, which has the city's most beautiful dining room. In the evenings, instead of balls or card games, they may go to a musical or out to dinner, followed by a dance at Annabel's or a flutter on the tables at Crockford's. Lord Byron would probably be as disparaging about their parties as he was about poor Charlotte Greville's.

Clockwork models of Messrs Fortnum and Mason come out to serve their public, accompanied by music, when the shop's clock strikes the hour.

ARTS AND ARISTOCRATS

'Just imagine, dear children, a street taking half an hour to cover from end to end, with double rows of brightly shining lamps ... and the pavement, inlaid with flagstones, can stand six people deep and allows one to gaze at the splendidly lit shop fronts in comfort. First one passes a watchmaker's, then a silk or fan store, now a silversmith's, a china or glass shop ... Just as alluring are the confectioners and fruiterers where, behind the handsome glass windows, pyramids of pineapples, figs, grapes, oranges and all manner of fruits are on show ...'

Sophie von la Roche, *Sophie in London*, 1775

STYLISH SHOPPING

Shopping in London has drawn foreign visitors for almost three centuries. Oxford Street offered variety and length, but the most select shopping was, and is, in St James's and Mayfair. The small but specialist shops of Jermyn Street include Turnbull & Asser the shirtmakers, Bates the hatters and Floris the perfumers (far left, top to bottom).

At the end of the eighteenth century, this area also benefited from the French invention of the shopping arcade. The modest Royal Opera Arcade (left), designed by John Nash and G.S. Repton and completed in 1818, enabled elegant ladies to browse in comfort on their way to Nash's now destroyed opera house. The high Victorian, grand Royal Arcade (right), completed at the end of the nineteenth century, was designed to lure shoppers walking from fashionable Brown's hotel to Bond Street.

THE PRINCE
REGENT'S LONDON

FROM REGENT STREET TO REGENT'S PARK, CAMDEN LOCK AND LITTLE VENICE

*'Among the magnificent ornaments of our metropolis
commenced under the auspices of his present Majesty,
while Regent, the Regent's Park ranks high in point of utility
as well as beauty, and is an invaluable addition to the comforts
and pleasures of those who reside in the north-west quarter of
London. A park, like a city, is not made in a day; and to
posterity it must be left fully to appreciate the merits of
those who designed and superintended this delightful
metropolitan improvement.'*

This eulogy in *The Times Telescope* reflected Londoners' delight in the dramatic improvements to their city. In 1825, when it was written, Regent's Park was nearing completion, as was the unashamedly grand triumphal approach to it, the mile- (1.5 km-) long Regent Street that sloped up from Carlton House in front of St James's Park. Carlton House itself, George IV's home when he was Prince Regent, was Regent Street's southern focus, but would be demolished the following year.

This whole project – which put London not merely on a par with Napoleon's Paris but well ahead of it in terms of the width of its streets – was the realization of a dream shared by two men: the young, enlightened Prince Regent who acted as patron, and his elderly but flamboyant architect, John Nash. Until now, London had grown piecemeal in response to the needs of the commercial City of London and the political and aristocratic City of Westminster. The laying out of Regent's Park and Regent Street was the greatest piece of order ever brought to London, changing its whole character and influencing its subsequent growth. Nothing on such a scale has happened since.

Three events created the catalyst. In 1811, the leases on Marylebone Park reverted to the Crown; Prince George became Prince Regent

Sussex Place (previous page) was one of several stucco terraces Nash designed as the backdrop to Regent's Park. Built in 1822, the year before he began work on the Royal Pavilion at Brighton, its octagonal domes and polygonal bay windows display a similar eccentricity. Nash's Regent Street (right), leading to Regent's Park, still hums with the quality shops for which it was designed. At Christmas, shoppers are lured by the decorations and lights.

after his father, the popular George III, was declared insane; and the tide began to turn in the Napoleonic War of 1803-15, thanks to Wellington's victories at Victoria and Waterloo. The mood in London was upbeat, another building boom began, and now London had a royal patron of refined taste.

But what of the two men at the heart of the project? The Prince Regent had left St James's Palace when he came of age in 1783. Setting up home in modest Carlton House, he soon enlarged the house to palatial proportions, imbuing it with good taste, and introducing an air of high spirits in the shape of his bright Whig circle of friends – the Carlton House Set. The handsome, curly-haired Prince of Wales entertained lavishly and often, as his figure would soon show. He lived here for about thirty years with no proper role in life, squandering a fortune on marble from Siena to adorn his home, on a garden which stretched as far as Marlborough House, on furniture bought by special agents sent to France and China, and on an inordinately extravagant lifestyle.

One of his grandest parties was held on 19 June 1811, to inaugurate his Regency. From that moment, as *de facto* king, he had a role. He had power, too, and used it partly to become the only British royal to make a direct, profound and lasting impact on London's landscape.

John Nash was a perfect partner for the Prince Regent. Physically, the two men were opposites. Nash described himself as a 'thick, squat, dwarf figure, with round head, snub nose and little eyes', far removed from the handsome prince. The son of a Lambeth millwright, he tried his hand at speculative building in Bloomsbury, went bankrupt, then retired to Wales. Later, he worked with the landscape gardener Humphrey Repton, who introduced him to the Prince of Wales. He was soon in tune with the Prince's taste. And thanks to the Prince's patronage, Nash was assured of wealth and influence. He married a woman who is thought to have been the Prince's mistress, and set up home in Mayfair's Dover Street.

It was a romantic vision matched by personal commitment that enabled these men to bring such radical change to London. The Prince's energy, extravagance and imagination, together with Nash's ability to create theatrical grandeur, provided London with Regent's Park and the great sweep of Regent Street. This was architectural unity on a breathtaking scale whose style – a mixture of gentle Classicism and the Picturesque – perfectly captured the novelty-seeking mood of the moment.

The whole idea of a triumphal street on a grand scale was new. Similarly, the concept of an elite garden city – a park dotted with the elegant villas of the rich which would include the Prince's own summerhouse – was new. And just as the grand plan was innovative, so were many of its details. The streets were to be wider than elsewhere in London, designed to carry aristocrats' carriages from the exclusive residential areas of Westminster, St James's and Mayfair to the new park. The use of stucco was a novelty too, bringing an almost dazzling whiteness to London's fast-expanding, mostly brick-built façades.

Nash's Regent Street set off from Carlton House's French-style colonnade. Small streets and alleys were swept away to create a monumental square, now Waterloo Place. Then, to outdo Paris's Rue de Rivoli, Regent Street sliced through Henry Jermyn's St James's development, compensating the people emerging from Charles II Street with an impressive new façade for the Theatre Royal. This stage-set effect – which often took little account of the soundness of the structure behind the stucco – continued at Piccadilly Circus. Here, Nash persuaded the County Fire Office to base their building on Inigo Jones's façade for old Somerset House. Today, despite a new front and the banks of neon lights, the effect is still good.

The next section of Regent Street, the great curve and long sweep up to Oxford Street, was triumphant in its boldness and would for ever divide the gentry of Mayfair from the workers of Soho. Work began in 1817, when 700 Soho buildings and many streets were destroyed. Londoners, amazed, watched what was described by a contemporary as 'a most extraordinary scene of digging, excavating, burning, and building . . . more like a work of general destruction than anything else'. By 1823, it was almost complete. But Nash was by then in difficulties and had had to finance the curving colonnade himself. Some plots were bought up by his friends to help him out; others remained empty. Finally, attempts at uniformity had to be abandoned when storekeepers demanded custom-built façades.

Beyond the Oxford Street crossing, Nash closed the vista with All Souls' Church, then took Regent Street round the corner to Portland Place. A speculative street built by Robert Adam in the 1770s, Portland Place is 125-feet (38-m) wide and is one of London's grandest streets. It is also home to one of London's best-known buildings, Broadcasting House, since 1931 the headquarters of BBC radio.

Portland Place entirely suited Nash's needs. He linked it to a huge crescent – Park Crescent – to reduce the impact of the Marylebone Road and to emphasize the importance of Regent Street. Across the Marylebone Road he built Park Square East and West as the grand entrance to his idealistic garden city.

Regent's Park, first monastic lands, later a royal hunting ground, was ploughed up by Cromwell then leased to farmers after the Restoration. It was these leases that reverted to the Crown in 1811. Nash took the 472 acres (190 hectares) and, ignoring the fashion for squares, looked to his country-house work for inspiration, transforming the land into a pastiche of a nobleman's country estate. His dream was to have fifty-seven villas set among undulating hills planted with decorative clumps of trees, and provided with a lake, zoo and other quality amusements. The idyllic retreat was to have a romantic backdrop of panoramic terraces on three sides, with the Prince Regent's house looking towards the grandest – Cumberland Terrace.

Even though Nash's utopia was not completely realized, today's Londoners can revel in his vision. The landscaping is still there, as is the boating lake. Half a dozen of the fifty-seven villas were built – Decimus Burton's The Holme was the first, and recently a few more have been added. Above all, the panoramic terraces are there, seen across the wide expanses of green grass, and as romantic and impressive as Nash had intended. Hanover Terrace is all Nash; for Cornwall Terrace he was helped by Decimus Burton; Kent Terrace, built last, faces outwards; and Cumberland Terrace has been deemed 'the most breathtaking architectural panorama in London'.

In the park every season is special: in spring you can count the ducklings on the lake; in summer you can walk among the blooms of Queen Alexandra's Rose Garden; in autumn you can enjoy the sharp air and the leaves turning colour; and in winter you can watch a hearty Sunday game of football. And, to supplement London's theatre life, the park also has an open-air theatre where, on summer evenings, stage effects compete with the screeches and squawks of birds and animals wafting across from the zoo to the north.

The north side of the park does not have a terrace backdrop: its boundary is instead marked by the Regent's Canal. Although short, this was a vital connection between the terminus of the Grand Union Canal, which came down through the industrial Midlands to Paddington in west London, and the international Port of London. It opened in 1820 – when Nash floated down it in the City's state barge – and was soon the busiest stretch of canal in Britain. Even after the railways killed off most canal traffic, this section carried building materials for London's unstoppable expansion.

Nash's park stimulated fashionable development at Primrose Hill and beyond. To the west, St John's Wood grew up, and to the north, Chalk Farm and Belsize Park linked the fashionable hilltop villages of Hampstead and Highgate to the centre of town.

Camden, to the east of the park and the focus of canal life today, was a different story. Too far away to attract City gentry, at first it was covered with cattle pastures. But, as was often the case in London, it was an aristocrat who saw the area's potential. John Pratt, 1st Earl Camden, began building around 1800, but development of Camden and of Kentish Town remained modest until the arrival of an extra stretch of Regent's Canal with its timber and coal wharves. Today, the pretty, small-scale houses of Camden have been gentrified, and the weekend market for crafts, clothes and antiques that once huddled beside Camden Lock stretches right up the High Street and into Chalk Farm Road like one continuous, informal street party.

Cecil Thomas's 1950s bust of John Nash (opposite), architect of London's Regency redevelopment, is in the porch of Nash's All Souls' at Langham Place (1822-4). Cherubs gaze out from capitals supporting the portico (above).

NASH'S TERRACES

By the time Nash died in 1835, he had totally transformed a large part of London. His imposing yet elegant sweeps of harmonious Neoclassical streets and terraces impressed Londoners and foreigners alike.

Park Crescent (left), with Portland Place, linked the northern end of Regent Street and Regent's Park. Originally planned as a circus, only half was built. Work started in 1812 but the builder went bankrupt. In 1818, three other builders completed the crescent.

Chester Terrace (right) was built by James Burton in 1825 to Nash's design. It overlooks the eastern side of Regent's Park. Nash originally planned to put a statue on top of each of the terrace's fifty-two Corinthian columns, but decided the effect would not be good, so withdrew the idea.

After bomb damage during the Second World War, both crescent and terrace needed restoration. They were originally intended as houses for the rich, but today only Chester Terrace fulfils that function. Park Crescent accommodates a student hostel and offices.

'Augustus made it one of his proudest boasts, that he found Rome of brick, and left it of marble . . . The reign and regency of George the Fourth have scarcely done less, for the vast and increasing Metropolis of the British empire: by increasing its magnificence and its comforts; by forming healthy streets and elegant buildings, instead of pestilential alleys and squalid hovels; by substituting rich and varied architecture and park-like scenery for paltry cabins and monotonous cow-lairs . . . and, by beginning and continuing with a truly national perseverance, a series of desirable improvements, that bid fair to render London the Rome of modern history.'

James Elmes, *Metropolitan Improvements*, 1827

NASH'S PARK FOR THE PRINCE

The grand design for an idyllic park dotted with villas, devised by the Prince Regent and his architect John Nash in 1811, quickly generated other building in the area.

While the park was in its initial planning stages, Marylebone was already expanding rapidly and needed a new parish church. St Mary's, designed by Thomas Hardwick, was begun in 1813. Its imposing façade, with a grand Corinthian portico, looks straight through York Gate into Regent's Park. The fine circular tower (right) has a ring of free-standing columns above which gilded caryatids support the dome.

Surrounding and enclosing the park, Nash's stucco terraces began with Cornwall, Sussex, Hanover and Clarence (1821-3), continued with Ulster, York, Chester and Cumberland (1824-7), and ended with Kent facing out westwards, and Gloucester in the north-east corner (1827), whose red-painted pediments (above) are surmounted by Classical figures.

Central London Mosque (above), the principal mosque for Britain's two million Muslims, is a recent addition to Nash's Regent's Park. It stands near Decimus Burton's Hanover Lodge, on land given by Britain to the Egyptian government in exchange for land in Cairo. Sir Frederick Gibberd and Partners – whose other London buildings include Coutts' bank in the Strand and parts of Heathrow Airport – won the competition for the design. It was then 'arabized' to follow Middle Eastern conventions and built in 1972-8. Its glowing copper dome rising above the park's trees adds an extra touch of fantasy to Nash's designs.

The Mosque's imams have all studied at Al-Azhar University, Cairo, but the faithful who respond to the call to prayer issued from the soaring minaret come from all Islamic countries of the world. Arabic is the eighth most widely spoken language in London.

LITTLE VENICE AND MAIDA VALE

Regent's Canal (left) is silent today, the loads formerly carried by its barges now taken by rail or road. A handful of fishermen and locals stroll along the towpaths, while pleasure boats chug between Camden Lock and Little Venice. Some passengers hop off at Regent's Park where they may visit the zoo or climb Primrose Hill to enjoy the splendid views over London and explore its village of brightly painted stucco houses.

Little Venice in west London is a pretty oasis of immaculately kept, grand houses shaded by mature trees. In Formosa Street, the Prince Alfred pub (overleaf, left) was built around 1890. It has a number of tiny bars, known as snugs, to maintain lady visitors' privacy because at the time it was built pubs were considered unsuitable places for ladies. Heavy drinking was a constant problem in Victorian London and cabmen were famous for their drunkenness. The taxi drivers' shelter in Warwick Avenue (overleaf, right) is a rare survivor of the sixty-four shelters built by philanthropists as refuges for drivers to rest and enjoy a cheap meal and a non-alcoholic drink.

During the nineteenth century, London's population rose from 1.8 million to 6.5 million. Public transport was revolutionized to serve the thousands who teemed into the metropolis daily or who crossed its ever-expanding vastness. In 1836 the first railway opened; in 1863 the world's first urban underground railway was inaugurated. Different lines opened in quick succession to create a clean, fast transport system beneath the turbulent London streets. In 1907, the Bakerloo Line opened, financed by an American, Charles Tyson Yerkes. Middle-class Maida Vale, whose large houses adjoined Little Venice, was part of the line's extension in 1915. The highly stylized entrance to its underground station (overleaf, centre) survives, faced with red-glazed tiles and bold white lettering on black blocks.

WEST LONDON PARKS
AND MUSEUMS

KENSINGTON, HOLLAND PARK, SOUTH KENSINGTON AND NOTTING HILL

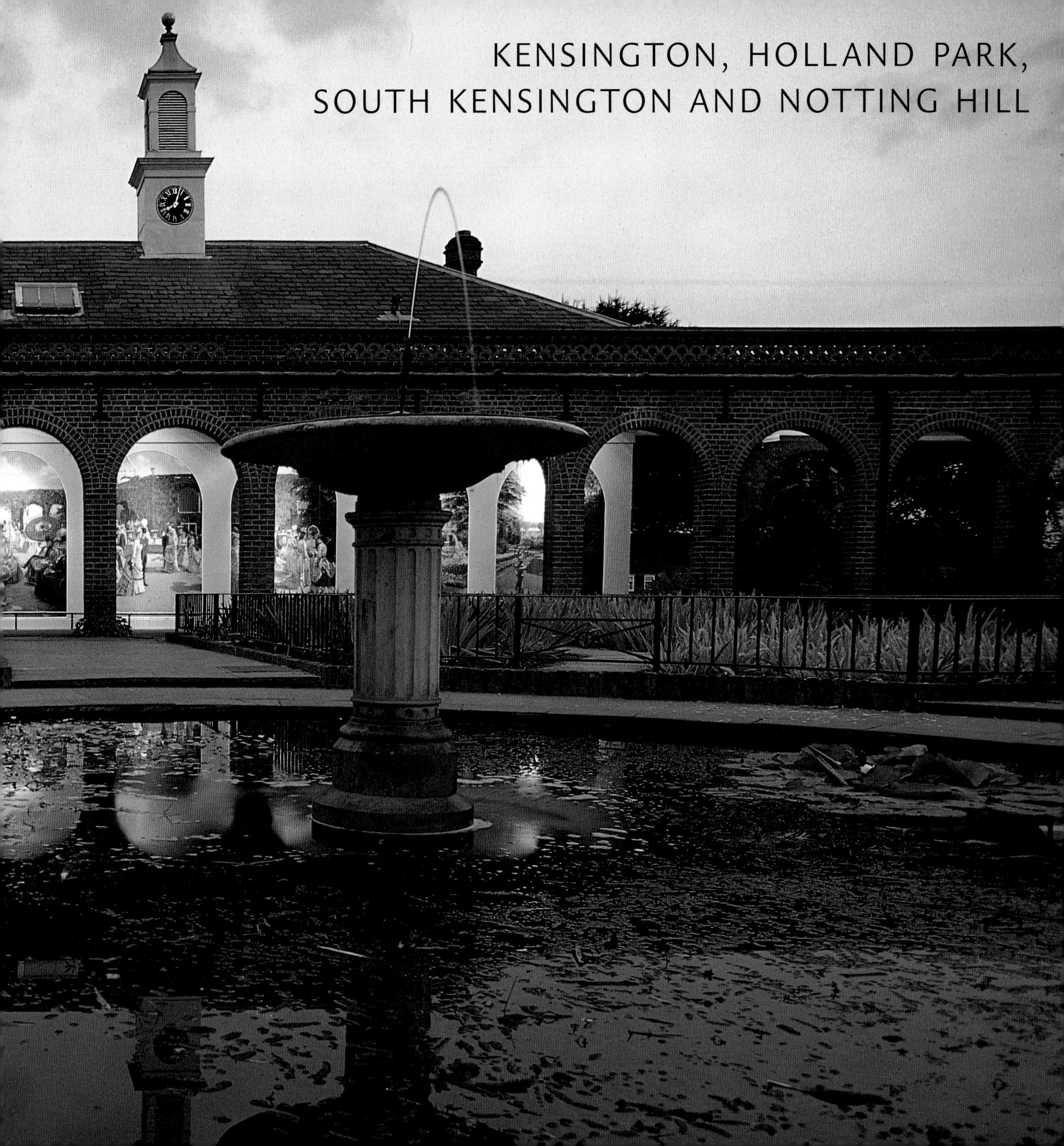

'The sight as we came to the centre where the steps and chair were placed, facing the beautiful fountain, was magic and impressive. The tremendous cheering, the joy expressed in every face, the vastness of the building, with all its decorations and exhibits, the sound of the organ (with 200 instruments and voices, which seemed nothing) and my beloved husband, the creator of this peace festival 'uniting the art and industry of all nations of the earth', all this was moving, and a day to live for ever. God bless my dear Albert, and my dear Country, which has shown itself to be great today . . . This day is one of the greatest and most glorious of our lives.'

So wrote Victoria the Queen-Empress in her diary on 1 May 1851 about the opening of the Great Exhibition of the Works of Industry of All Nations held on the south side of Hyde Park. Her pride in her husband Prince Albert's crowning achievement was fully justified. He was the inspiration and energy behind this vast celebration of Victorian dynamism – 100,000 exhibits from 13,937 exhibitors, of whom about half were from Britain and its world-encircling Empire. On the first day, 25,000 ticketholders thronged the Crystal Palace, the glass, cathedral-like hall that covered 19 acres (8 hectares) and dwarfed the trees it enclosed. When the exhibition ended on 15 October, six million people had visited it, a sixth of the whole population. Queen Victoria herself went forty times.

Using the considerable profits from the exhibition, Prince Albert became the driving force behind plans for a more permanent showcase for the arts and for industry on the fields south of Hyde Park. He dreamed of a cultural campus that would provide free learning for all people. His dream comprised colleges for the arts and sciences, lining an avenue that would lead to a huge national gallery, with museums and learned societies, concert halls and gardens beyond. But the National Gallery would not budge from Trafalgar Square. What was built instead was the Royal Albert Hall at the top of the slope in Kensington Gore, surrounded by colleges and societies that ranged from the Royal Geographical Society to the Royal College of Art. The Royal College of Music and what was to become the Imperial College of Science and Technology

were lower down; and the Science and Natural History Museums and the Victoria & Albert Museum were at the bottom, in Exhibition Road and Cromwell Road. This last, devoted to art and design, and the world's largest museum of decorative arts, has an encyclopaedic collection that is still growing. When the museum was rebuilt, Queen Victoria herself laid the foundation stone in 1899, and statues of her and her 'dear Albert' were placed either side of the entrance.

Prince Albert's cultural campus was to become the nucleus of yet another London development – South Kensington. Before the colleges and museums were completed, houses were being built in a variety of vibrant Victorian styles from the familiar Regency stucco to red-brick Queen Anne revival. Albert was never to see any of this.

Prince Albert, from Saxe-Coburg-Gotha, had been Queen Victoria's closest adviser since their marriage in 1840. He worked ceaselessly for his adopted country and after the Great Exhibition staged other similar exhibitions in Dublin, Manchester and London. Finally, in 1857, Parliament acknowledged his contribution and gave him the title Prince Consort. Four years later, aged forty-two, he died of typhoid. His project for a cultural campus was barely under way. The Queen withdrew into seclusion and never wholly recovered, while the Prime Minister, Benjamin Disraeli, told a stunned public: 'This German Prince has governed England for twenty-one years with a wisdom and energy such as none of our Kings have ever shown.' It is thanks to Prince Albert's foresight that London has a cultural hothouse at South Kensington. In George Gilbert Scott's elaborate Albert Memorial in Kensington Gardens, the prince sits holding a copy of the catalogue of his Great Exhibition, looking down with pride on his 'Albertopolis'.

The Orangery in Holland Park (previous page), built 1638-40, is now a restaurant. It was originally a fashionable garden room, housing orange trees and providing a well-lit, warm and large space for taking a stroll. Resembling a glazed loggia, its fine brick exterior is punctated with large windows. The Royal Albert Hall (left) stands on the main axis of the South Kensington cultural centre. Built in 1867-71 and inspired by the Roman amphitheatres of southern France, the great domed building was designed by Captain Francis Fowke. Its terracotta frieze depicts The Triumph of Arts and Letters.

THE NATURAL HISTORY MUSEUM

The Natural History Museum (1873-81) was Alfred Waterhouse's first public building in London. Born in Liverpool in 1830 into a Quaker family, Waterhouse trained as a Classical architect before converting to the Gothicism expounded by Pugin, Scott and Ruskin, and then set off to study Gothic buildings as far east as Constantinople.

In 1860, the Trustees of the British Museum resolved 'that it is expedient that the Natural History Collection be removed from the British Museum' to save money. Sir Richard Owen, the collection's creator and first director, and Captain Francis Fowke, who had designed the Royal Albert Hall, put together a plan to build a suitable storehouse for these wonders of creation. On Fowke's death, Waterhouse, recently moved to London, inherited the plan. Keeping much of it intact, he changed its style from Italian Renaissance to the more robust Romanesque.

The monumental style gives the building its cathedral-like personality: the central hall is its nave, while the exterior has the towers, spires, arches and columns of eleventh- and twelfth-century Rhineland churches. The honey, cream and grey-blue terracotta of the exterior was new to London and provided a forceful contrast to the Victoria & Albert Museum next door. It also fulfilled Waterhouse's aim that colour should 'make our buildings effective, even under a gloomy sky'. Being also cheap, resistant to acid and easy to wash, terracotta was ideal as a building material in a smoke-filled Victorian city.

Round-arched windows run the whole length of the 680 feet (207 m) of the façade overlooking Cromwell Road. The western part of the building is decorated with models of living birds and beasts, the eastern part with extinct ones, reflecting the layout of the galleries inside.

'My earliest recollections are connected with Kensington Palace where I can remember crawling on a yellow carpet spread out for that purpose – and being told that if I cried and was naughty my "Uncle Sussex" would hear me and punish me for which reason I always screamed when I saw him.'

Queen Victoria, 1872, quoted in William Gaunt, *Kensington*

Queen Victoria mostly remembered her childhood at Kensington Palace (left) with affection. Built between 1661 and 1702 by William and Mary, Kensington Palace looks more like a large family home than a royal palace. 'Never did any powerful monarch of the age', wrote architectural historian Nikolaus Pevsner, 'build a less ostentatious palace.' Kensington Gardens adjoin the palace, opened fully to the public by Queen Victoria in 1841. Among the statues added to the gardens since then is George Frampton's bronze Peter Pan *of 1912 (right). Set in a small dell beside the Long Water, the child hero stands on top of a tree trunk clustered with rabbits, mice, squirrels and ethereal fairies. Nina Boucicault, star of J.M. Barrie's 1904 play,* Peter Pan, *is thought to have been the model for this statue, but its composition is largely taken from Barrie's* The Little White Bird *which he wrote about Kensington Gardens.*

With her visits to the Great Exhibition, Queen Victoria found herself close to Kensington Palace, which had been her childhood home. Here she was born on 24 May 1819 and lived until, scarcely aged eighteen, she became Queen on 20 June 1837. Three weeks later she moved to Buckingham Palace, on the threshold of a sixty-four-year reign during which Britain's commercial and political power reached its zenith. But Victoria did not forget her childhood home. It was she who opened all its gardens and state apartments to the public in 1841. Later, in 1901, her son Edward VII fulfilled her wish when he made Kensington a Royal Borough.

But it was an earlier king and queen – William and Mary – who first gave rural Kensington its royal associations. They and the eighteenth-century Hanoverian rulers who followed were responsible for early developments in the area. In 1689, the year William and Mary came to the throne, they left Westminster for Kensington. The dank air by the river at Whitehall Palace aggravated William's asthma: Kensington's fresh air and open countryside were far preferable. The King and Queen bought Nottingham House near the small village of Kensington, and brought in Sir Christopher Wren and Nicholas Hawksmoor to reconstruct and enlarge it. They also partitioned off an adjoining piece of Hyde Park to indulge their gardening hobby, and laid out a formal Dutch garden there. With its red-brick walls and small rooms, unostentatious Nottingham House – soon renamed Kensington Palace – would remain one of the official London residences of the ruling sovereign until 1762, when George III left for his newly acquired Buckingham House. Since then, a string of royal relatives has moved in and out.

In 1696, during its early years, the diarist John Evelyn visited Kensington

Palace and found it 'very noble, tho not greate; the Gallerys furnished with all the best Pictures of all the Houses, of Titian, Raphel, Corregio, Holben ... and others, with a world of Porcelain; a pretty private Library; the Gardens about it very delicious'. To the 'delicious' gardens, Queen Anne added the Orangery and some English character, while George I improved the 'very noble' house, employing Colen Campbell to design the great staircase and state rooms, and William Kent to decorate them. This work was completed in 1727. Queen Caroline, George II's wife, focused her attention on the gardens and enlarged them by enclosing more of Hyde Park.

Today, in this most atmospheric and domestic of all London royal palaces, Queen Mary's bedchamber can be visited, along with Kent's glorious painted ceilings and rooms filled with Princess Victoria memorabilia. There is a room devoted to Albert's Great Exhibition, with a silver table centre made for the occasion by the royal jeweller Garrard and incorporating portraits of Victoria's four dogs.

The 275-acres (111-hectares) of Kensington Gardens retain the private aura of aristocratic childhood, quite different from the thoroughly public Hyde Park. They were first opened by George II, to 'respectably dressed people' on Sundays only: no soldiers, sailors or servants were allowed. Now, children sail their boats on the Round Pond and play among the sculptures, follies and ancient sweet chestnut, red oak and ash trees. They walk beside Queen Caroline's Long Water, with its weeping willows and mallards, and seek out George Frampton's statue of Peter Pan, J.M. Barrie's fictional boy who never grew up. Queen Anne's Orangery is now a tea-room, while the uniformed nannies who once pushed well-sprung prams along the paths have been replaced by health-seeking joggers and teenage rollerbladers.

THE QUEEN MOTHER'S GATE

A glowing red lion and white unicorn leaning against a blossoming tree of life full of exotic birds forms the central focus of the Queen Elizabeth Gate (right), installed at the south-east entrance to Hyde Park in 1993. It honours Her Majesty Queen Elizabeth the Queen Mother's lifetime of service for the nation and the Commonwealth – symbolized by the British wren and Indian peacock. Prince Michael of Kent was inspired to commission the gate after seeing what he described as 'the great show of public affection generated on the occasion of Her Majesty's 90th birthday' in 1990.

The Queen Mother was born Lady Elizabeth Bowes-Lyon on 4 August 1900, at 21 St James's Square. In 1923 she married Prince George, known as 'Bertie', second son of George V, at Westminster Abbey. They had two daughters, Princesses Elizabeth (later Queen Elizabeth II) and Margaret. When Edward VIII abdicated on 11 December 1936, his younger brother Bertie became George VI. His wife, therefore, became Queen Elizabeth, his consort, until his death in 1952.

Rather than reflecting her interests in fishing and horse-racing, the gate honouring Her Majesty keeps to a floral theme, showing her passion for gardening. Giuseppe Lund designed and built it, while the centrepiece was sculpted by David Wynne, whose works scattered round the capital include *Girl with a Dolphin* by Tower Bridge.

THE SERPENTINE

It was Queen Caroline, an extravagant and energetic gardener, who in
1730 annexed a chunk of Hyde Park to Kensington Gardens and began
her project to divert the Westbourne stream and to create the Long Water
in Kensington Gardens and the Serpentine in Hyde Park. In 1930, the
Lido (above) was built; many Londoners swim there in the summer and
some brave ones take a dip on Christmas Day. During the Second World
War, pipes were built, ready to use the water for fighting fires caused by
the Blitz. Today, in an echo of royal eighteenth-century outings, visitors
can hire rowing boats (left).

Framed by lawns and woodland, the Serpentine is visited by a wide
variety of waterfowl. In summer, flocks of mallard, tufted duck, pochard,
coot, moorhen and Canada geese are readily visible, whereas sharper eyes
are needed to catch sight of the spotted flycatchers and herons. In winter,
cormorants and shovelers make their appearance.

When the monarchs left Kensington Palace for Buckingham House, the gardens' continuing popularity as a fashionable rendezvous helped Kensington village sustain its up-market development. During Victoria's reign, terraces of gleaming stucco, inspired by Nash's work for the Prince Regent, spread westwards over Notting Hill and down its slopes. In the 1840s, to the south, the network of delightful streets around Victoria Road, Launceston Place and Albert Place were laid out as Kensington New Town.

These streets contrast sharply with Kensington Palace Gardens, a road laid out at the same time over the royal vegetable gardens to the west of the palace. It was a tree-lined avenue 1½ miles (2.5 km) long, lined with vast, opulent mansions that made some of Mayfair's look modest. This was grandeur on a scale London had not seen since Nash built Regent Street and Regent's Park. It was soon nicknamed 'Millionaires' Row', but most of its millionaires have now been replaced by ambassadors.

While Kensington High Street is today a focus for some of London's big stores as well as for streetwise fashion and novelties, the streets either side of it retain their traditionally select residents. Leafy Kensington Square is surrounded by handsome houses mostly built in the eighteenth century by courtiers drawn here by William and Mary's move to Kensington.

Across the High Street, a network of roads runs up the hill to Campden Square. James South lived in Campden Hill Road, where, in his garden in 1831, he erected the world's largest telescope. West of here, a generation later, the fields of the Phillimore Estate were transformed into tidy, gleaming terraces. Here, artist Linley Sambourne's over-stuffed late Victorian home survives intact as a museum run by the Victorian Society.

If it were not for Holland House and Holland Park, the developers would have surged on unhampered. The earliest manor house on this spot was William I's gift to Aubrey de Vere in thanks for his loyalty. Several centuries later, Holland House – a rare Jacobean house built in 1606-7 – was bought by Henry Fox, Paymaster General, with money he made from speculating with public funds. At the beginning of the nineteenth century, his grandson, the 3rd Baron Holland, inherited and made Holland House the centre of Whig politics and literature. Here, Sheridan, Palmerston, Macaulay and Dickens contributed to a court that was more influential than the King's, and was openly supportive of the French Revolution.

When Baroness Holland's lavish entertaining forced her into selling some of the land belonging to Holland House in 1866 and 1873, three streets of imposing houses to be called Holland Park (above) were built on it for the newly wealthy of Victorian London. With their dazzling white stucco finish and elaborate iron canopies, they remain among London's most exclusive addresses.

George Godwin's colourful, painted stucco terrace is in Priory Walk (overleaf), hovering between South Kensington and Fulham. The stylized Italianate windows, pediments, balconies and doors are picked out in brilliant white. Godwin was also the architect for the nearby Boltons – two crescents of palatial stucco mansions facing each other.

The next generation of Hollands preferred grand and glittering balls to stimulating conversation. To fund her lavish lifestyle the 4th Baron's widow sold off two parcels of land in 1866 and 1873. Thus began the development around Holland House and its 45-acre (18-hectare) park of lawns, terraces, summer theatre and woodland. The area to the north was laid out in 1866 as an estate of eighty-seven immensely grand formal houses with elaborate ironwork, on three roads all confusingly called Holland Park. To the south, the development was dramatically different. These leafy roads became an enclave of dream houses for rich, successful artists. The exotic Arab Hall of Frederick Lord Leighton's home in Holland Park Road, now a museum, epitomizes the Aesthetic Movement that flourished in England at the end of the nineteenth century. Leighton and his neighbours – architect Philip Webb, Pre-Raphaelite painter William Holman Hunt, and others – employed the most dynamic architects of the day, among them Richard Norman Shaw, George Aitchison and Halsey Ricardo, to design their homes, while the architect William Burges built himself a Gothic dream in the area.

North of Holland Park, a mixture of farms, potteries and piggeries covered the slopes of Notting Hill until the Victorian developers, keen to supply houses for London's fast-expanding middle class, arrived. Here, royal clockmaker Benjamin Vulliamy sold his 50-acre (20-hectare) Norlands Farm which, in the 1840s and 1850s, became a small-scale estate centred on Norland Square.

James Weller Ladbroke had more ambitious plans for his Notting Hill Farm. He envisaged a Utopian garden city of large villas with private gardens opening on to communal gardens. Work was slow and the plan was only partly realized, the main change being that after Ladbroke's death in 1850 the villas were replaced by more economical terraced houses. Despite this, once complete in 1870, the Ladbroke estate became London's most spacious Victorian estate with architecture of the highest quality.

But this area has never been just an enclave for the rich. By the end of the nineteenth century, gypsies were trading horses and herbs along the track down to another farm, Porto Bello. Soon, there were Saturday-night markets here, and after the Second World War, antiques dealers from the now-closed Caledonian Market came to trade here instead. Today, Portobello Road's Saturday antiques market is one of Britain's longest, spilling into side streets and along Kensington Church Street.

DEBENHAM HOUSE

Debenham House (above and left), also known as Peacock House, at 8 Addison Road, Holland Park, was built between 1905 and 1907 by Halsey Ricardo for Sir Ernest Debenham. His fashionable department store, Debenham and Freebody, was one of the first Post Office subscribers, and glorified in the telephone number 'Mayfair One'.

With Debenham House, Ricardo, a member of the serious-minded Artworkers' Guild, added a notable building to a corner of London already favoured by successful, wealthy artists. George Aitchison had designed an exotic Italianate house (1864-6) for the aesthete Lord Leighton in Holland Park Road. Its Arab Hall is decorated with tiles collected during Leighton's eastern travels. Philip Webb designed Val Prinsep's studio next door and William Burges designed his own Gothic house on Melbury Road, where the Pre-Raphaelite painter William Holman Hunt and the Dickens illustrator Marcus Stone later also lived.

Debenham House is a masterpiece of coloured ceramics both inside and out. Every surface of the exterior is made of Burmantofts Staffordshire brick and Doulton tiles – even the capitals and cornices are moulded and glazed, as is each small piece that makes up William de Morgan's phoenix medallion in the attic (left). While the arcade, attic and chimneys are covered in white tiles, the infill panels of green-glazed bricks on the lower floors and of blue-glazed bricks in the attic symbolize garden and sky respectively. This gives the house a light, transparent quality.

'Carnival time was on Saturday nights in winter . . . when it was thronged like a fair . . . the people overflowed from the pavements so that the roadway was quite impassable for horse-traffic . . . On the left-hand side were costers' barrows, lighted by flaming naphtha lamps. In the side streets were side-shows.'

Sir William Bull, 1870, quoted in
Kevin Perlmutter, *London Street Markets*

PORTOBELLO ROAD MARKET

When Sir William Bull wrote his description of Portobello Road's market, it was already a place where commerce and entertainment met. Named after the Caribbean city of Puerto Bello, captured by Admiral Vernon in 1739, the road tumbles down the hill from Notting Hill Gate to Golborne Road.

Today, the Saturday market stretches so far that it is really several markets. At the Notting Hill end, the established antiques shops and their stalls sell the more expensive goods – only the knowledgeable will pick up a real bargain here. Down the hill, northwards, less ambitious bargain hunters can strike lucky, then pause in the pubs and cafés to show each other their finds. Farther down, beyond Westbourne Grove, are areas for second-hand clothes and bric-à-brac. Finally, there is a fruit and vegetable market in Golborne Road, and beyond that second-hand bicycles, household goods and new clothing are sold.

This area is home to London's Caribbean community, immigrants from the Commonwealth countries who arrived in London after their countries won independence from British rule. Now, every year in August, at Carnival time, decorated floats, steel bands and dancing fill the streets.

EMBASSY HEARTLAND TO
RIVERSIDE VILLAGE

BELGRAVIA, PIMLICO, KNIGHTSBRIDGE AND CHELSEA

CHELSEA WHARF

'The West End of London was in those days partitioned into a number of distinct residential districts ... The very rich and fashionable lived in Mayfair, Belgravia, Park Lane; the artistic, literary and bohemian gravitated towards Chelsea or even Bloomsbury; Hampstead, Hammersmith and St John's Wood were middle-class; while the substantial London houses of run-of-the-mill squires, knights, baronets and barons were found in Kensington, Paddington, Marylebone and Pimlico. We were in the last category.'

Long before 1960, when Jessica Mitford wrote these words in her book *Hons and Rebels*, London had become a city divided by class. In Queen Victoria's reign, the class distinctions became acute. Victorian London, capital of Britain and of an empire that included a quarter of the world's population, had expanded greedily over any space it could find, checked only by the royal parks, its lungs of green open space and recreation. During the nineteenth century, its population increased substantially, partly because of the arrival of immigrants. Some were Irish, fleeing the Irish Potato Famine of 1847-8; others were Jews, fleeing anti-Semitic pogroms in Russia and Poland in the 1880s. Many of them moved to the East End, where they lived in poverty. But the number of wealthy Londoners grew too, and with that growth came demand for homes in west London, which was more salubrious than the overcrowded East End, and where the rich could be as close as possible to their monarch. Developers were quick to answer these demands. Mayfair and St James's had reached full capacity during the eighteenth and early nineteenth centuries so, by arrangement with Lord Grosvenor who

The Thames (previous page) twists and turns as it flows through London, presenting infinite views – of boats and bridges, warehouses and homes, towers and chimneys, all speaking silently of the city's past. One landmark riverside building is the Tate Gallery, where a statue of Sir John Everett Millais (opposite) shows the Pre-Raphaelite painter holding his palette and looking out over the water. Behind the Tate lies elegant Belgravia. Here Seth Smith's sweeping Wilton Crescent (right), with giant pilasters typical of this development, was built in 1827 as a grand entrance from Hyde Park to Belgrave Square, the centrepiece of the Grosvenor estate.

owned the land, the marshes hard by Buckingham Palace garden wall were drained. Over the next thirty years, this land would be covered with the classical stuccoed streets and squares of Belgravia. It would be the last of the London estates to be developed by the rich for the rich.

The design of Belgravia – which gave traditional Georgian plans a new Regency splendour, scale and spaciousness – was by James Wyatt and Thomas Cundy the Elder. The gleaming squares, crescents and terraces of this unashamedly up-market, 200-acre (80-hectare) enclave, which was twice the size of Mayfair, had the effect of moving the centre of London society and influence farther west. The development also sealed the fate of Knightsbridge and linked Chelsea with London.

Building began in 1824. Two of the three major builders went bankrupt; the one who did not was Thomas Cubitt. Cubitt had revolutionized building methods: instead of contracting trades separately for each job, he employed all his workmen on a permanent wage and created the first modern building firm in London. He boldly took the lease on the development's centrepiece – Belgrave Square – which would be London's largest square so far, and also built Upper Belgrave Street, Eaton Place and the more intimate Chester Square. Digging up the marshy clay, Cubitt baked it into bricks for building and filled the holes with good soil from his firm's St Katharine's Dock project on the far side of the City, transporting this soil up the Thames by boat.

Belgravia's success was both instant and long-lasting. In the 1850s, Mrs Gaskell praised it effusively: 'Behold that desert now – a gorgeous town!' Smart society moved from Mayfair to Belgravia and in many cases stayed; today, the owner of Mayfair and Belgravia himself, the Duke of Westminster, lives in a flat in Belgravia. After the First World War, when some aristocrats began to give up their Belgravia mansions in order to maintain their country homes, foreign missions moved in. More than twenty great houses in and around Belgrave Square

are now embassies and consulates, including those of Austria, Germany, Saudi Arabia, Syria, Portugal, Spain and Malaysia.

Cubitt continued the stunning success of his Belgravia work in Pimlico. In 1835, he took a lease on all the available low-lying marshy land south of Belgravia, tucked into a bend of the Thames. Here, over the next thirty years, he laid out Pimlico's squares and terraces, less grand but more harmonious than Belgravia's. This is the largest area of London to have been built by one man.

Sold off by the Grosvenors, Pimlico was subsequently cut off from Belgravia by Victoria Station. Today its friendly atmosphere is reinforced by small, local shops in Warwick Way and Wilton Road, and by a lively street market in Tatchbook Street. Down beside the Thames, Pimlico's local museum is the airy Tate Gallery. Its International Modern collection is being rehoused at Bankside, leaving the British collection behind in the renamed National Gallery of British Art.

The development of Belgravia also stimulated that of Knightsbridge. During the eighteenth century, smart Piccadilly divided St James's and Mayfair, but then continued as a rough road leading out of town past small villages. The first of these villages was Knightsbridge, where the road divided for Kensington and South Kensington. In the 1820s, Knightsbridge was surrounded by more than 600 acres (240 hectares) of market gardens and fields. Its rise started with a cluster of small-scale, stuccoed Regency lanes begun in 1818 by Arthur Trevor Hill and soon frequented by army officers from the local barracks visiting their mistresses. Boosted by the Great Exhibition of 1851, more development took place in the second half of the century. A new character was stamped on the area in the shape of large-scale Victorian squares such as Rutland Gate, whose mews houses built as stables are now the dolls'-house homes of the wealthy. Later, the style of building in the area turned from Classicism to a revival of English vernacular architecture known as the Queen Anne style.

'It is difficult nowadays to realize
how very personal was then the
relationship, even in London, between
shop-keeper and customer and the
enormous importance, comparable
almost to that attained by rival
churches, which late Victorian and
Edwardian ladies attached to certain
stores. All my female relatives had
their own favourites, where some of
them had been honoured customers
for more than half a century and their
arrival was greeted by frenzied bowing
on the part of the frock-coated
shopwalkers, and where certain of
the older assistants stood to them almost
in the relationship of confessors,
receiving endless confidences on the
state of their health, the behaviour of
their pets and the general iniquity of
the Liberal Government.'

Osbert Lancaster, *All Done from Memory*, 1963

WEST LONDON SHOPPING

Knightsbridge was, and still is, the commercial hub of the new, up-market west-London area that grew up after the Great Exhibition of 1851. Its character is epitomized by the rise and rise of Henry Charles Harrod's grocery shop, now housed in Stevens and Munt's splendid Edwardian building (opposite), constructed 1901-5. Behind the terracotta tiles and sparkle of fairy lights, staff serve more than 35,000 customers each day, hoping to live up to their motto: '*Omnia, omnibus, ubique*' – 'everything, for everyone, everywhere'.

The Scotch House, opened in 1830, and Harvey Nichols, started as a draper's shop by Benjamin Harvey in 1813, have enjoyed similar success. And top architects have remodelled some of the lucrative fashion shops in Knightsbridge – Eva Jirinca designed shops for Kenzo and Joseph, and Stanton Williams was responsible for the Issey Miyake shop.

South of Knightsbridge lies the ever-changing Sloane Square (right), first laid out in the 1750s. Gilbert Ledward's 1953 bronze Venus fountain is one of the square's twentieth-century additions. Peter Jones, the department store, is behind it, built 1936-8 on the corner of King's Road. This street enjoyed its heyday in the Swinging Sixties, when London was the essence of trend-setting and prosperity, described by *Time* magazine as 'seized by change, liberated by affluence'. King's Road was synonymous with the Beatles, Mary Quant, miniskirts for girls and long hair for men – all rejected wholesale in the 1970s by the Punk movement. Today, King's Road is still Chelsea's backbone, and the London catwalk for the latest street fashion and youth culture.

Today, Chelsea appears to be interwoven with Knightsbridge. But its origins are very different; for Chelsea already had a substantial history by the time Knightsbridge was built.

Chelsea's main highway, the King's Road, was, from the time of Charles II's restoration in 1660 until the 1830s, part of the private royal route to Hampton Court, Kew and other aristocratic country retreats. Indeed, some aristocratic homes were in the King's Road itself. Tudor mansions stood in Chelsea when, in 1681, Sir Christopher Wren built the Royal Hospital alongside Ranelagh Gardens. Sloping down to the Thames, these gardens now host the annual Chelsea Flower Show – Britain's biggest and most competitive. But Ranelagh Gardens have seen more louche times. In the eighteenth century they rivalled the infamous Vauxhall Gardens as a fashionable pleasure resort, 'full of fetes, frolics, fire-works and fashionable frivolity'.

During this time, Sir Hans Sloane, an obsessive collector whose artefacts formed the core of the British Museum collection, bought the Manor of Chelsea from the Cheyne family in 1712 and came to live in it in 1741. Sloane, a successful physician, may not have visited the pleasure gardens, but he certainly supported and studied at a more serious garden near by. This was the Society of Apothecaries' 4-acre (1.5-hectare) Chelsea Physic Garden, whose medicinal plants and trees were shipped in from around the world and arrived at the wharves of the old Chelsea fishing village.

Sloane also made other contributions to Chelsea, including giving six chained books to Chelsea Old Church. After his death in 1753, his manor house was pulled down and the houses of Cheyne Walk were erected by his son-in-law, Baron Cadogan of Oakley.

So began Old Chelsea, which survives today as a maze of lanes. Later, in the 1830s when Chelsea's luck was down, the Scottish historian and philosopher Thomas Carlyle came to live in Cheyne Row. He found his new neighbourhood 'unfashionable; it was once the resort of the Court and great, however; hence the numerous old houses in it, at once cheap and excellent'.

At Chelsea Embankment, houses convey the illusion of still being at the water's edge, while onlookers can imagine themselves in the old fishing village far from town that Chelsea once was.

'Here [in Chelsea] is the
Noblest Building, and the
best Foundation of its kind
in the World, viz. For the
Entertainment of Maimed
and Old Soldiers. If we
must except the Hospital
call'd des Invalids at Paris,
it must be only that the
Number is Greater there,
but I pretend to say that the
economy of the Invalids
there is not to compare with
this at Chelsea; and as for
the Provisions, the Lodging,
and Attendance given,
Chelsea infinitely exceeds
that at Paris. Here the Poor
Men are lodg'd, well
cloathed, well furnish'd,
and well fed.'

Daniel Defoe, *A Tour Thro' the
Whole Island of Great Britain,*
1724-7

CHELSEA RESIDENTS

Sir Christopher Wren's Royal Hospital, Chelsea (left), built 1681-91, looked to Louis XIV's Les Invalides in Paris for inspiration. Today it still houses army veterans as originally intended. Its 400 pensioners proudly wear their distinctive red uniforms.

Farther west, the immaculate houses of Park Walk (right) are typical of many brick terraces lining Chelsea's streets. They were built from the late eighteenth century onwards for London's fast-expanding middle class. Streets like these surrounded and then replaced the earlier country palaces until finally the distinction between the core riverside fishing village and the sprawl of London was lost. Relatively modest, these houses, with their narrow façades, have standard sash windows and deep internal rooms with brick party walls. They were, in essence, a form of mass-production housing. Today, however, they are considered some of London's most desirable addresses.

The combination of these 'cheap and excellent' Georgian houses and the Thames light found at the quiet riverside village of Chelsea attracted not only writers such as Thomas Carlyle and later Oscar Wilde, but also painters such as Whistler, Holman Hunt, Sargent and Turner. A different sort of tone was set in 1862 at No. 16 Cheyne Walk when Algernon Swinburne, George Meredith and Dante Gabriel Rossetti and his zoo – including some noisy peacocks – all moved in. Old Church Street has houses designed in the 1930s by Erich Mendelsohn and Serge Chermayeff and by Walter Gropius and Maxwell Fry. Today it is the wealthy patrons of art rather than impoverished artists who can afford to live in Chelsea.

The 1870s proved to be pivotal for the area. First, Sir Joseph Bazalgette's second plot of land reclaimed from the Thames was developed, creating Chelsea Embankment. With a road above ground and a sewer below, the embankment cut Chelsea off from the river, while Thomas Page's Chelsea Bridge and R.M. Ordish's Albert Bridge, later overhauled by Bazalgette, connected Chelsea to the fast-growing south bank suburbs over the water.

The architect Richard Norman Shaw found Chelsea Embankment the ideal place to build Cheyne House, Old Swan House and others in the new red-brick Queen Anne revival style. Taking its inspiration from English vernacular architecture of the sixteenth and seventeenth centuries, the Queen Anne style marked the first real break with late-Georgian classicism's uniform façades, porticoes, columns, classical details and white stucco finish.

This new domestic urban style was at the heart of the second great change Chelsea underwent in the 1870s. The Cadogan family, descendants of Sir Hans Sloane, still owned large tracts of the area. Ignoring the public outcry as they swept away street after street in Hans Town, they replaced housing for the 'respectable poor' with housing for the rich, using the Queen Anne revival style; the new buildings were tall, red-brick, with balconies and richly decorated doorways. With this new Hans Town development, the Cadogan family succeeded in linking Chelsea to Belgravia and luring the wealthy farther west. One contemporary observed when Cadogan Gardens and Cadogan Square were almost complete: 'What a surprise it is to be taken to Sloane-street ... the red-brick houses now being all but completed ... the houses of dear old friends replaced by magnificent mansions for, if not magnificent people, the possessors certainly of magnificent means'.

'[In 1915] I went to live in Cheyne Walk, Chelsea, at the shabby end, then the home of working artists. From there I looked out on to the power station chimneys and Turner sunsets ... Life in Chelsea suited me. I had begun to abandon bourgeois styles of dress ... it has always been customary for "arty" people to dress for beauty or bizarre effect rather than for fashion. We made our own clothes, at this time peasant-style pinafore dresses of vivid cretonne, over a very bright, coloured blouse.'

Dora Russell, *The Tamarisk Tree*, 1975

Named after Lord Cheyne, who owned this stretch of the river bank before it was developed in the eighteenth century, the handsome houses of Cheyne Walk form a living museum of three centuries of fine domestic architecture. Its long list of remarkable former residents, many of whom were artists and writers, includes the writer George Eliot at No. 2, the Pre-Raphaelite painter Dante Gabriel Rossetti at No. 16, and J.M.W. Turner, who lived and died at No. 119.

RIVERSIDE HOMES

Chelsea's riverside location has inspired the decoration of its buildings and streets. Swans – given royal protection on the Thames – appropriately decorate the front doors and oriel windows of Old Swan House (right). Designed by Richard Norman Shaw in 1876, it was built on the newly completed Chelsea Embankment and is the finest of a cluster of houses designed in the Queen Anne revival style. The appeal of Queen Anne buildings was their quiet elegance, simplicity and intimacy, in marked contrast to the Palladian grandeur of the columns and stucco that characterized recently built Belgravia and Pimlico near by. Behind the gentle red brick and white woodwork of Old Swan House, the interior was decorated by William Morris, who was called in by the owner, connoisseur Wickham Flower.

David Wynne's bronze sculpture, *Boy with a Dolphin* (left), stands at the bottom of Oakley Street, opposite Albert Bridge. Made in 1975, its clean lines and graceful movement are typical of Wynne's many public works in London. Three of his bronzes may be seen in neighbouring Belgravia: *Girl with Doves* stands in Cadogan Place's south garden, *The Dancers* in the north gardens and *Dancer with Bird* in Cadogan Square.

STREET SCULPTURE

In addition to their many other advantages, the 32 acres (13 hectares) of land reclaimed by Sir Joseph Bazalgette when he engineered the Thames embankments provided London with new sites for sculptures. The street furniture for the embankments set the tone: Egyptian sphinxes and sitting camels for bench supports (right) and twisting dolphins for the lamp-posts. In the Chelsea section, Francis Derwent Wood's nude bronze, *Atlanta* (above), was erected by his friends three years after his death in 1926. It stands at the end of R.M. Ordish's Albert Bridge, constructed in 1871-3 and later overhauled by Bazalgette.

NORTH LONDON
VILLAGES

*'One cannot be at Kensington without visiting Hamsted, three Miles off, on the Brow of a Hill,
from whence you have the fullest View of London. It is a large and pleasant Village . . . Its nearness
to London brings so many loose Women in vampt-up old Cloaths to catch the City Apprentices,
that modest Company are ashamed to appear here even with their Relations . . . adjoining to
this Village the Duke of Argyle hath a fine Seat called Caen-Wood.'*

So wrote John Macky in his *Journey Through England* in 1714, the year George I came to the throne, a year that ushered in 116 years of Georgian rule. It was to be a time of extreme affluence and expansion for London, and a period of enlightened culture for many of its inhabitants. Already some wealthy people, with their households and service industries, were moving westwards towards the City of Westminster and the Court, which was based at St James's and then at Kensington Palace. Their migration caused the growth of St James's, Mayfair and Kensington, and was ultimately to inspire the development of the whole of residential west London.

But Londoners of all classes felt the need to escape the muggy Thames basin on summer evenings and holidays. Their nearest resorts were to the north, up the hills to the fresh air, pure waters and jolly entertainment of nearby Islington or farther out to Hampstead and Highgate.

In the nineteenth century, as London expanded, what had been undeveloped land became the new suburbs. The fields and farms that once gave the villages their out-of-town holiday appeal were now covered with new housing. Just as west London had extended to include Holland Park and Notting Hill, so the land north of Regent's Park became the streets of Chalk Farm, Camden, Kentish Town and Belsize Park. Hampstead and Highgate were now firmly within reach of London's tentacles, saved only by Hampstead Heath lying between the two. Islington, lacking such a park, was throttled by London's rapacious expansion – the market gardens of Georgian Islington and Hackney were transformed into Barnsbury, De Beauvoir Town and Stoke Newington.

In the twentieth century, north London suffered from social decline. The city's population, 2.5 million in 1850, hit 10 million in the 1930s and 1940s, creating pressure on housing. North London's Victorian houses were often divided into flats for workers and even the grander Georgian ones became down at heel. Although some people maintained genteel households – Evelyn Waugh and George Orwell were among the writers who enjoyed the seedy gentility of Canonbury – many middle-class families joined the mass exodus of a million Londoners to the suburbs.

Today, Islington, Hampstead and Highgate are riding high on the crest of a fashionability that took off in the 1970s and gained momentum in the 1980s. Their new residents are a similar mix as in Georgian times – artists, writers and intellectuals, with a growing number of City merchants. They have restored the fine houses and brought new life to the entertainment business that originally made the villages famous. Restaurants and shops abound, theatres and markets thrive, and every street has its lively residents' association.

*The slopes of Parliament Hill Fields look towards Highgate Hill (previous page) and Hampstead. Acquired for the
public in perpetuity in 1887, the hills are part of rambling Hampstead Heath, the precious green lungs for north Londoners.
In Hampstead's tight-knit streets, Church Row (right), built in 1720, is a perfect Georgian terrace complete with ironwork,
while an eagle (above) guards Romney House, built in 1797 for the painter George Romney.*

Although Islington, Hampstead and Highgate have their similarities, each has its own story. Islington, now unashamedly urban, began as the nearest bolt-hole from the City. It lies just north of Clerkenwell which, just outside the City walls, was already famous for its springs of sweet water by the twelfth century – indeed the area was named after one, Clerk's Well. Islington developed later. Its Tudor mansions with lush gardens, dairy farms and market gardens were fed by even purer spring water. Its future was sealed when, in 1684, its curative springs were compared favourably with those at Tunbridge Wells in Kent. More convenient than Kent, Islington became a favourite resort for eighteenth-century Londoners. Its many visitors included George II's daughters, who came to take the waters which apparently cured all ailments including 'Hysterics, Vapours, Dropsies, Swellings of the Legs'. To enliven people's stay, Islington offered lime walks to wander in, public breakfasts to feast on, and the inevitable dancing and gambling. The spas multiplied, each becoming a magnet for entertainment of all kinds. Sadler's Wells was one, its adjoining music-room becoming a theatre in the mid-eighteenth century.

In the nineteenth century Islington began to change. A string of informal Regency and Victorian squares covered the orchards and gardens. These started with Myddleton Square in 1827 and continued with Barnsbury, Lonsdale, Cloudesley, Gibson, Milner and finally Thornhill Square, completed in 1852.

While the developers were amassing their fortunes, Islington was changing fast. Two main high roads from the north and north-east ran into London here. In 1862 the Royal Agricultural Hall opened to house the live cattle market that had moved from Smithfield. This gave a boost to the pubs, and markets that were already thriving, and encouraged more music halls and theatres to open.

Today, Upper Street, the old road leading north, still lies at the heart of Islington. Chapel Market off Upper Street sells fruit and vegetables, while nearby Camden Passage, saved from developers, is full of antiques shops and, twice a week, a crush of stall-holders. The King's Head, Old Red Lion and Almeida are among almost a dozen fringe theatres in the area. There is also the rebuilt and revived Collins Music Hall, where cattle-dealers used to come and let their hair down over a good sing-song. As for places to eat and drink, Upper Street now has more cafés, bars and restaurants than any other similar street in Europe.

Lloyd Square (right) provides spectacular views westwards to the 580-feet- (180-m-) tall Telecom Tower. This hilltop square is the charming centrepiece of the modest Lloyd Baker estate, developed from 1819 on the steep fields rising from King's Cross to Islington. They lay near Bagnigge Wells, a popular eighteenth- century spa where Nell Gwyn and her lover Charles II were said to meet to sip water and enjoy the orchestra, water temple, bowling-green and distorting mirrors.

Thomas Lloyd Baker employed a father-and-son team, John and William Joseph Booth, as architects. In the face of fierce local opposition, they built some remarkably individual houses, luring City professionals with the rural character of the villas and gardens. But with the coming of the railways in the 1850s, the estate lost some of that character and therefore its prestige. Houses were let as lodgings, and it was only in the 1970s, after the Lloyd Baker family sold half the estate to the local council, that the area began to rise again.

Amwell Street, one of the estate's main roads, still boasts many old shops such as Lloyd's Dairy (left) at No. 42. This is an echo of the days when Welsh cattle were fattened up in the area before being sold in London, and Welsh families ran the local dairies.

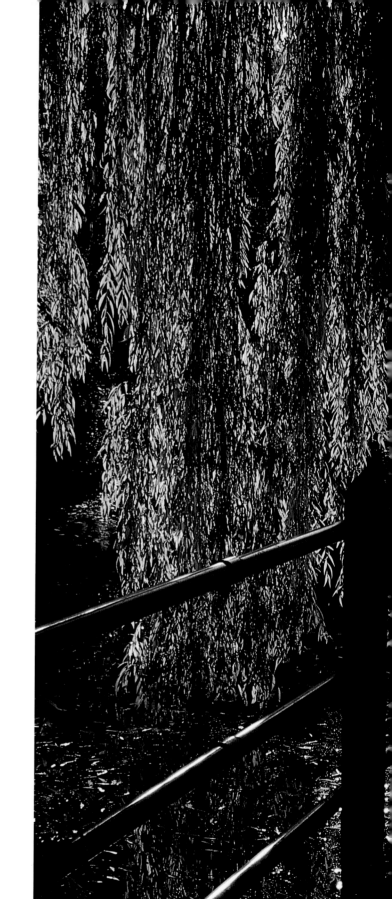

NEW RIVER WALK

A green oasis in parkless Islington, New River Walk (right) runs alongside the canal built by Sir Hugh Myddleton to bring fresh water from the River Lea in Hertfordshire to the City. Opened in 1613, the triumphant project left an enduring mark on Islington.

During the Georgian building boom, Islington lost many of its mansions, orchards, dairies and vegetable patches to rows of handsome, flat-fronted, simple terraces. One exceptionally long pair of terraces, Colebrooke Row and Duncan Terrace (above), face each other across the New River. Colebrooke Row was begun in 1710, Duncan Terrace followed at the end of the century. Later, the arrival of Nash's Regent Canal through the 970-yard- (900-m-) long Islington Tunnel in 1820 brought new industry, trade and a flood of residents, for whom a chain of Victorian squares was built.

'For all my dislike of Hampstead thinkers and their thoughts, I have lived in Hampstead twice myself. I too have walked her winding streets and lanes and peered into her umbrageous gardens where rich progressive ladies sit under the trees and plan to overwhelm South Africa with blood and fire. I too have tramped her noted heath in all weathers . . . I have hated Hampstead for her Left-wingery, but I have loved her for her strange, secret, leafy soul. Nowhere in London are green thoughts so green, especially in a rainy June, when the grass grows high in her innumerable gardens tamed and wild.'

Michael Wharton, *The Stretchford Chronicles*, 1980

Roses, pink foxgloves and a smoky blue mass of campanula ramble through a Hampstead cottage garden in Flask Walk (left). This pedestrian lane of delightful eighteenth-century cottages leads off Hampstead High Street. Its name harks back to the time when flasks were bought at the nearby Flask public house and filled with water from Hampstead Wells. Promoted as being 'of the same nature and virtue as that of Tunbridge Wells', the water was sold in City pubs for 3d. a flask. During Hampstead's heyday as a fashionable resort and through its later, more disreputable years, artists and intellectuals from Hogarth to Karl Marx strolled up Flask Walk to meet friends for a pint. One early group who met there were the Kit-Kat Club, founded in 1700 by Whig politicians and writers to ensure a Protestant succession at the end of William III's reign.

The urban buzz and fast pace of Islington are quite different from the leafy tranquillity of Hampstead and Highgate, both of which retain something of the rural atmosphere that first attracted Londoners. Of the two, Hampstead takes the prize. With its intellectuals and café society, handsome red-brick homes and immaculate lanes of pretty cottages leading to the vast expanse of Hampstead Heath's woods and grassland, it has the edge over Highgate, which lies quietly on the other side of the Heath.

Both villages started to prosper in the sixteenth century. Their fresh, hilltop location directly to the north of Westminster and the City was favoured by successful merchants, who built villas that enjoyed impressive views of London. One later visitor described the area as possessing 'a most extensive and varied view over Middlesex and Berkshire, in which is included, besides many inferior places, the majestic Windsor and lofty Harrow'. Against this benefit must be set the fact that travel into town from Hampstead and Highgate was by road, which was considerably less safe than by boat along the Thames, the preferred means of transport into London from other fashionable country districts such as Greenwich, Richmond and Twickenham.

During the eighteenth century, Hampstead's golden age ran parallel with Islington's. Farther away from London's seething masses and the filth of the Thames basin, Hampstead, with its health-giving waters, was considered the more select pleasure resort. But while in 1714 John Macky recommended travellers not to miss its 'fullest View of London' and its 'large and pleasant Village with Mineral Waters as at Tunbridge', he clearly judged the wicked City to be responsible for the less savoury behaviour of some visitors. Others, drawn there for 'exercise and harmless merriment' as they deemed it, felt differently. Hampstead's taverns and bowling greens multiplied and there was even a racecourse.

As the fame of Hampstead's 'sweet salutarie airs' and its springs spread, so the modest village expanded around its handful of substantial houses. The wealthy, the artistic and the intellectual flocked to live here – politician William Pitt, poet Lord Byron, architect George Gilbert Scott, writers Robert Louis Stevenson, D.H. Lawrence and John Galsworthy, and many more. The Russian ballerina, Anna Pavlova, who in 1907 created the role of Fokine's Dying Swan, kept swans in her Hampstead garden.

For nineteenth-century artists, such as John Constable, who lived in Well Walk, Hampstead perfectly combined nature on an expansive scale with retreat and study, while still being within easy reach of London: 'Our little drawing-room commands a view unsurpassed in Europe . . . The dome of St Paul's in the air seems to realize Michelangelo's words on seeing the Pantheon: "I will build such a thing in the sky." ' Indeed, the prospects from Hampstead were so impressive that public houses would erect special viewing steps. Today a gazebo beside Kenwood House contains a map identifying the buildings caught in that particularly fine view.

Whereas Islington's past lives on in its markets and entertainments, Hampstead's lives on in these views and in the several homes that belonged to past celebrities and are now open to the public. Fenton House is one, a fine William and Mary building of 1693; Burgh House is another, where Hampstead physician Dr William Gibbons lived in splendour on his profits from tending the ailing. In 1818, the Romantic poet John Keats moved into an unpretentious house in Keats Grove, and was perhaps inspired to write 'Ode to a Nightingale' after hearing the songbird as he sat beneath a plum tree in his garden. His house is now a museum, as is that of psychoanalyst Sigmund Freud, who in 1938 escaped from war-torn Vienna and came to the tranquillity of Maresfield Gardens.

Heath Street is the main thoroughfare of Hampstead village. The lanes, alleys and mews leading off it, such as Flask Walk, Well Walk and Church Row, are so pristinely maintained they seem to be ready for use as the set of a costume drama. South of Heath Street, Hampstead Square is lined with Georgian mansions. And it is in picture-perfect Hampstead that the National Trust has two of its small collection of protected London properties: one is the group of Georgian cottages of Squire's Mount; the other is 2 Willow Road, designed and built by Erno Goldfinger in 1939.

Other remarkable homes are to be found in Highgate. Some surround pretty Pond Square; others are strung along the steep High Street, where magnificent Georgian houses are interspersed with discreet shops. And Lauderdale House, built well down Highgate Hill in 1660, is now open to visitors, who can also enjoy the azaleas and mature trees in its grounds, now Waterlow Park.

At the bottom of the park, Highgate Cemetery, opened in 1839, is one of London's most interesting and best-kept graveyards. Among the Egyptian obelisks, stone angels and ornate catacombs there are memorials to poet Christina Rossetti, writer George Eliot and political philosopher Karl Marx.

NORTH LONDON PUBS

The pub-owners of Hampstead and Islington did well out of travellers to and from London, and resident Londoners escaping the overcrowded, dirty city for a few hours. Built in 1643, Holly Bush Tavern (left) took over the stables of the painter George Romney's house in 1807, when the house became the Assembly Rooms. Its name derives from the custom of hanging a green branch or bush over a door to advertise the sale of wines or beer.

The name of another Hampstead pub, The Wells Tavern (right, below), obviously derives from this spa village, although it was at first called The Green Man and only changed its name in 1850. It stands in Well Walk, which for the first twenty years of the eighteenth century was the focus of Hampstead's rise as a spa resort. Here was the Great Room, containing the Assembly Room for dances and concerts, and the Pump Room for drinking the health-giving local waters – both highly fashionable until gambling discredited the whole building.

The Freemasons Arms (far right) stands at the heath end of Downshire Hill, a street of delightful Regency houses built in the early nineteenth century by William Woods. Founded around 1820, it was built over one of London's many lost rivers, the River Fleet which runs down from Hampstead to Holborn. Until recently, its gardens contained England's last pell mell court. This was the game, similar to croquet, that Charles II so enjoyed, and after which Pall Mall in St James's is named.

Standing on the main road north out of London, Islington has many old-established pubs. The Island Queen (right, top) in Noel Road opened in 1848, the year the street was completed. Standing near the wharves that follow Islington Tunnel, when the barges lost out to the trains in the 1850s this large building became a pub for locals.

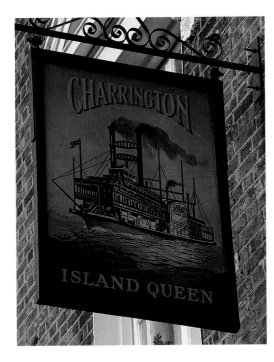

'No, Sir! there is nothing that has yet been contrived by man, by which so much happiness has been produced as by a good tavern.'

Samuel Johnson, *Boswell's Life of Johnson*, 1776

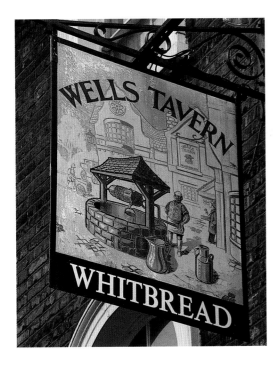

'There are a few fields just north of this parish of Marylebone . . . and there on a summer Sunday or Saturday evening you might see hundreds of working people . . . perhaps they go on up to Hampstead Heath, to which these fields lead, which many could not reach, if these acres were covered with villas . . . They are now like a green hilly peninsula or headland, stretching out into the sea of houses . . . Our lives in London are over-crowded, over-excited, over-strained . . . we all want quiet; we all want beauty for the refreshment of our souls.'

Octavia Hill, 'Space for the People', *Macmillan's Magazine*, 1875

HAMPSTEAD HEATH

Hampstead and Highgate's back garden is the Heath (left and right) that lies between them, tame today but once the home of highwaymen and wild beasts. This tract of open land is a testimony to the vigilance of small communities living in big cities. Just as the residents of Covent Garden saved their Piazza, and those of Islington saved Camden Passage, so north London locals fought off developers and 'improvers' to keep Hampstead Heath as an open space for all to enjoy. Today, north Londoners can visit their Heath, relishing 'the fullest View of London' as so many others have before them. They can roam the woods, climb the hills and enjoy sculptures and memorials such as the terracotta Goodison Memorial Fountain (left, below) erected in 1929. Or they can relax on the great sweep of nearby landscaped lawns crowned by Kenwood House.

KENWOOD HOUSE

The gleaming white mansion overlooking Hampstead Heath is Kenwood House. First built in the seventeenth century, it was remodelled in 1764-9 by Robert Adam for the hugely successful 1st Earl of Mansfield, who rose to become George III's Chief Justice. The Earl bought the Kenwood estate in 1754 to be his country residence when he was not at his town house in Lincoln's Inn Fields.

The view from it was magnificent even by Hampstead's standards: the previous owner, Lord Bute, wrote that 'the whole city with sixteen miles of River appears from every window'. Mansfield bought up all the surrounding land he could, so that by the time he died in 1793 he owned 232 acres (95 hectares), including Parliament Hill and Hampstead Ponds. Access to all of it was denied to the public.

Then change came. Between 1831 and 1871, local people fought a long battle with various owners. Bit by bit they won the right for the 789 acres (320 hectares) of Hampstead Heath to be kept 'for ever ... open, unenclosed and unbuilt on'. Parliament Hill was bought from the Kenwood estate in 1887 by public subscription and added to the Heath. London's kite-flyers gather here to perform deft aerobatics. Kenwood House itself, with Humphrey Repton's landscaped gardens, is one of north London's most ravishing free facilities. Edward Guinness, 1st Earl of Iveagh, bought it in 1925, filled it with fine paintings and then bequeathed the house, gardens and collection to the nation in 1927, making it the glory of Hampstead, Highgate and the Heath. The views from the South Terrace are as good as ever; there are pictures by Vermeer and Rembrandt, Gainsborough and Romney; Adam's glorious library, one of his masterpieces; and Repton's lake and gardens are the setting for summer concerts.

HAMPTON COURT, RICHMOND, KEW AND CHISWICK

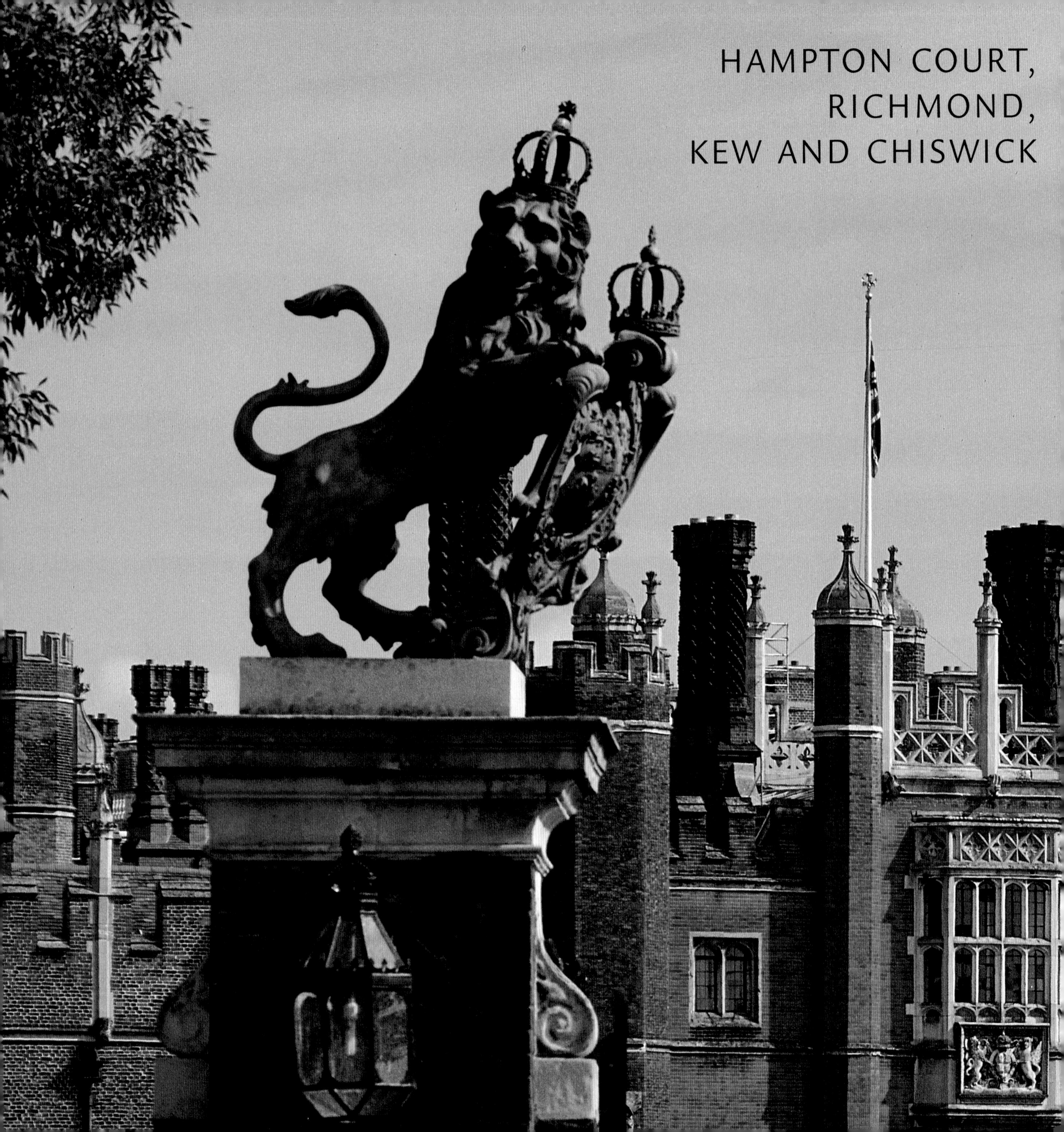

PALACES,
PROSPECTS
AND
VILLAS

*'From hence we came to Richmond, the delightful Retreat
of their Royal Highnesses, the Prince and Princess of Wales,
and where they have spent the fine Season every Summer for
some Years ... From Richmond to London, the River sides
are full of Villages, those Villages so full of Beautiful Buildings,
Charming Gardens, and Rich Habitations of Gentlemen
of Quality, that nothing in the World can imitate it.'*

Daniel Defoe's rhapsody in his *A Tour Thro' the Whole Island of Great
Britain*, written in 1724-7, was probably inspired by the view from
Richmond Hill, at that time one of the best known and most highly
praised prospects in the country. The eighteenth-century love of
'prospect viewing' led aristocrats to build villas on the high ground
around London – a villa being designed purely for pleasure as
distinct from a country house, which was an ancestral country seat.
Less spectacular or flatter sites could be enhanced – or indeed
transformed – into very fine prospects if they had an association
with the Thames or royalty, or preferably both. Hampton Court,
Richmond, Chiswick and Kew had the perfect credentials.

The area's royal links stretch back to Edward III. He and his
descendants lived at the palace of Shene, rebuilding and enlarging
it over the years. This was to become Henry VII's favourite palace,
rebuilt after a fire in 1499 and renamed Richmond after Henry's
earldom of Richmond. His grand-daughter Elizabeth I would spend
her summers here and coteries of courtiers – Cecil, Walsingham,
Leicester, Raleigh and Sidney – lived in the vicinity.

In 1514, another courtier, Thomas Wolsey, had bought a country
site at Hampton, well upriver from Richmond Palace. Here he began
building his uncompromisingly grand 280-room palace. Holding
the positions of both Cardinal and Lord Chancellor, he was then at
the summit of his meteoric career, dominating both church and
state. But in 1529, when he failed to win from Rome a divorce for the
heirless Henry VIII, he fell from favour. Henry took over Hampton
Court, moved in and enlarged it with courtyards, kitchens, a library,
tennis courts and a guard room. His daughter Elizabeth I made it
the 'most splendid' royal palace in England, while the Stuart kings
kept up the style, staging thirty plays there one Christmas and
enlarging the palace's magnificent art collection. William and Mary

brought in Sir Christopher Wren, still busy on St Paul's Cathedral, and began replacing the Tudor buildings and their playful chimneys with their dream of an English Versailles. Of Wren's plan, only the state apartments were built, their classic French Renaissance façades overlooking Charles II's older French-inspired gardens and William's Dutch ones. The Hanoverians, with their more sober lifestyle, enjoyed Hampton Court too, while it was Queen Victoria who first opened this largest and most spectacular of London palaces to the public.

Outside the grounds lie two more of London's royal parks – Home Park and Bushy Park. Hampton Court's grand fountains and the Long Water lead to Home Park, dotted with sheep which graze beside the Thames. Bushy Park, despite its formal avenue of magnificent horse chestnut trees, has a wilder feel to it. Its herds of fallow deer and clumps of rhododendrons make London seem far away.

Leaving Edwin Lutyens's elegant Hampton Court Bridge, built 1930-3, the river curves downstream round Home Park and passes through Kingston-upon-Thames. Teddington Lock and Weir mark the beginning of the tidal Thames. Twin towns follow: Twickenham on the west bank and Richmond on the east. Linking them are Richmond Bridge, built in the 1770s, the newer Twickenham Bridge, and a rare surviving ferry that carries visitors from the west bank to Ham House.

Although by the eighteenth century Richmond Palace was already a romantic ruin, nearby Ham House survives from Tudor times to give an idea of the scale of aristocratic spending. Built in red brick by Sir Thomas Vavasour in 1610, it was vastly enlarged and refurbished later in the century by Elizabeth, Countess of Dysart, and her husband, John Maitland, Duke of Lauderdale, to create a riverside English Baroque palace. Today, the rooms running around the double-height hall are fully furnished with the help of loans from the Victoria & Albert Museum.

Looking through the entrance gates to Hampton Court (previous page), visitors are greeted by a view of Cardinal Wolsey's Tudor palace. Walking on Richmond Hill (left) in 1727, James Thomson delighted in its 'goodly prospect'. The aristocracy built their idyllic country mansions here, artists painted scenes from the hill and of the hill, while more modest Londoners boated upstream on day trips. In 1902 the local council bought the land to preserve the view.

RIVERSIDE GRANDEUR

Today, many people – like the royal parties before them – arrive at Hampton Court by river, to be greeted by the view of the twelve-panel, wrought-iron screen and watergate (left) built for Charles II by Jean Tijou. After his restoration in 1660, Charles II spent much time in this rural haven – he chose to honeymoon at Hampton Court after his marriage to Catherine of Braganza in 1662, and brought his pictures here from Whitehall Palace during the Great Fire of 1666. Inspired by Le Nôtre's work at Versailles, he remodelled the 50 acres (20 hectares) of formal gardens to include fountains, cascades, avenues of limes and Tijou's gates. William and Mary, coming to the throne in 1689, further developed the Versailles dream. The view through the gates today shows their King's Apartments – totally restored since a devastating fire in 1986 – and their Dutch-inspired Privy Garden.

While Hampton Court is a blend of Tudor and eighteenth-century buildings, nearby Ham House (right), lavishly remodelled from 1672 onwards, encapsulates the flamboyant English Baroque. Even at a time when extravagance was excused after the austerity of the Commonwealth period, Ham's ostentation outside and inside was a matter for contemporary comment.

Standing beside the Thames at Petersham, just upstream from Richmond, Ham's warm red brick is enlivened with a variety of decoration: stone and lead busts adorn the north entrance with its Classical columns and frieze, while a Coade stone figure personifying the River Thames reclines in the formal gardens in front. Charles II's Portuguese bride, who came to stay here, would have been able to enjoy the remarkable seventeenth-century garden which survives today.

ROYAL HUNTING GROUND

London's largest and wildest open space is Richmond Park. Almost 2 miles (3 km) wide and covering 2,358 acres (954 hectares), it contains a rare surviving tract of the dense forest of oak, elm and lime trees that once covered London. When Charles I enclosed the park as a royal hunting ground in 1637, there were 1,600 fallow and 200 red deer. Today there are about 200 of each. In spring and summer, they graze quietly on the lush grass, but in autumn, when the rutting season starts, the throaty roars of the red deer stags carry across the park. Because of its size and its variety of natural environments – grassland, natural woodland, marshland, lakes and managed forest – the park is now one of the south of England's more important reserves. In addition to its fine trees and herds of deer, the forest plantation enables foxes, badgers, weasels and stoats to live in peace by day and to hunt by night. Coots, grebes, divers and other waterfowl live around the lakes, and winter visitors include flocks of Canada geese.

East of Ham House, in Richmond Park, George I built his Palladian house, White Lodge, in 1727, while George II, as Prince of Wales, was living at Richmond Lodge. This was around the time of Defoe's visit and his description of the 'Villages so full of Beautiful Buildings ... that nothing in the World can imitate'. George II continued to spend time at Richmond Lodge after becoming king, and employed Capability Brown to landscape the gardens there.

By then, the prospect from Richmond Hill had long been famous. In 1677 Ham House's Duke of Lauderdale had commissioned the painter Jan Siberechts to paint the view of his mansion from Richmond Hill. The hill drew crowds of people from London who also visited the nearby spa and, during George II's reign, could wander in Richmond Park, newly opened to the public. Artists came, to execute commissions for views of the new villas being built, or to study the effects of light there. Some artists even had homes in Twickenham and Richmond – Kneller, Hudson, Reynolds and others. Turner built his own villa there.

The house that would have stood out most in any view from Richmond Hill was Marble Hill, a fine white Palladian villa standing between Twickenham and Richmond. It was completed in 1729 for George II's mistress, Henrietta Howard, Countess of Suffolk. The house encapsulates the English Classical enlightenment with its rich allusions to the ideal of the Italian villa of the sixteenth-century Veneto and that of the ancient *campagna* of the Roman poets. Of other local villas, only Chiswick

House matches it. Marble Hill's park, designed by royal gardener Charles Bridgeman and Augustan poet Alexander Pope, was a classically inspired earthly elysium with carefully contrived views towards the busy river from the house and, equally importantly, towards the house from the river. The Countess maintained other close friendships, first with Pope, who at his nearby villa created his own garden, mixing 'beauty and ruin', and then with Horace Walpole, who in 1748 also came to live in the area, at nearby Strawberry Hill. When the Countess fell from royal favour, Walpole observed and wrote about her glittering alternative court at Marble Hill. Today, now that it is immaculately restored, it is easy to imagine Marble Hill in its heyday, particularly during a summer concert on the lawns.

The gracious terraces of Montpelier Row and Sion Row – built around 1720, before Marble Hill – marked the start of Twickenham's rise to popularity. Along the riverside path, Orleans House Gallery is all that remains of James Gibbs's palatial Orleans House, built around the same time. Later, in the nineteenth century, some of the parties who came to enjoy Richmond Hill's fine prospect would arrive by river steamer and pause at Twickenham to visit Eel Pie Island's tavern. Here, as vividly described in Charles Dickens's *Nicholas Nickleby*, they would enjoy beer, shrimps, eel pies and dancing.

Twickenham was a 10-mile (16-km) journey from central London. Downriver, round a wide bend of the still-rural Thames, lies Kew, a little nearer to London and much more accessible. Kew sits in an

Marble Hill House (above), completed in 1729, epitomizes the relatively modest Thameside pleasure villas built for the aristocracy.

oasis of rural England. The village green, with its church and fine surrounding houses, stands outside the Royal Botanical Gardens, while over Kew Bridge lie the pretty riverside cottages of Strand-on-the-Green. Inside the gardens the little royal palace was the force behind Kew's fashionability. Built in 1631 by a London merchant of Dutch descent, it was another Georgian favourite. In 1759, George III's mother, Princess Augusta, began the planting of its 9-acre (4-hectare) gardens. William Aiton was head gardener, Lord Bute botanical adviser and Sir William Chambers the architect – he designed the Pagoda visible from the Thames.

When George III inherited both the Kew and the Richmond estates, he preferred Kew Palace to White Lodge, and employed Sir Joseph Banks to enlarge the gardens. Banks, who had been round the world with Captain Cook, sent gardeners to collect specimens from all continents. Later, the gardens were given to the state and were further enlarged. Sir William Hooker, the director from 1841 to 1865, founded the Department of Economic Botany and the museums, Herbarium and Library. Today, the Royal Botanical Gardens at Kew are the foremost botanical research centre in the world.

A view easily missed, but surely not by the prospect-viewers of the eighteenth century, is the one from inside Kew gardens across the Thames to magnificent Syon House, outside Brentford. This is no pleasure villa. Since the sixteenth century, Syon has been the sumptuous seat of the Northumberland family, whose equally impressive town mansion stood at the Westminster end of the Strand until it was demolished to create Northumberland Avenue. The shell of old Syon House survives, but the interior was totally remodelled by Robert Adam in 1761 for Sir Hugh Smithson, the 1st Duke. Adam controlled the entire project, from the building and fine plasterwork to the gilding, carpet designs and furniture. Charles Fowler designed the huge conservatory that was added in 1827, linking the house to its 55 acres (22 hectares) of Capability Brown's landscaped gardens. Today, the meadow of the London Butterfly House in the grounds of the house continues Syon's garden tradition.

At nearby Isleworth, away from the river, Robert Adam remodelled yet another aristocratic country seat – Osterley Park. An Elizabethan house had been built here by Sir Thomas Gresham, the great merchant who founded the Royal Exchange in 1566. Sir William Chambers made some alterations. Then Adam, starting in 1761, totally transformed Osterley Park for those later City successes, the bankers Francis and Robert Child. The Childs' Palladian elysium even included tree-filled pleasure grounds dotted with Classical garden temples.

The river is still essentially rural as it meanders on down-river to Chiswick, but London's presence begins to be more keenly felt. Riverside streets such as Chiswick Mall were already being built when one of London's leading arbiters of taste, Richard Boyle, 3rd Earl of Burlington, was creating his exquisite villa, Chiswick House, in the neighbouring fields. Lord Burlington was an immensely refined and influential connoisseur whose town house on Piccadilly pioneered the move away from Wren's English Baroque to Palladio's lighter, Italian version. At Chiswick, which he conceived as a country villa to display his art treasures and entertain his friends, Burlington created his idea of Palladian perfection: the house was modelled on Andrea Palladio's Villa Capra ('Villa Rotunda') near Vicenza. William Kent advised on the interior and the garden. Work began in 1725 and the building was completed four years later.

Since Lord Burlington's day, London has almost engulfed Chiswick Park, so that it now stands out like an island of green. It is hard to imagine William Hogarth choosing to live here in the summers of the 1850s and 1860s because of the open fields.

A lion, representing the Northumberland family, tops the much-altered battlemented façade of Syon House (above).

KEW GARDENS

The 300 acres (121 hectares) of the Royal Botanical Gardens at Kew have their origins in a dolls'-house-sized palace, the gardens surrounding it and a chunk of the park of Richmond Palace. Today, these gardens, enclosed by bends in the River Thames, are a living museum of plant specimens, landscapes, garden buildings and statuary.

A stone lion wearing a royal crown lies in front of the eccentric, ten-storey Pagoda (left) designed by Sir William Chambers in 1761 and originally decorated with eighty enamelled dragons fixed to the corners of its balustrades. Although usually a classical architect – he designed Somerset House at Aldwych – Chambers travelled extensively in China. His other works at Kew, all now destroyed, were a Chinese temple, a Moorish Alhambra and a Turkish mosque.

William E. Nesfield, whose father laid out Kew's four great vistas – Pagoda Vista, Broad Walk, Holly Walk and Cedar Vista – designed one of London's first Queen Anne revival buildings in 1866-7: the delightful Temperate House Lodge (right), whose tall central chimney has fine detailing.

Kew has many fairytale glasshouses. The slender cast-ironwork of the great Palm House (overleaf, top left), designed by Decimus Burton and Richard Turner in 1844-8, makes this the finest existing glass and iron structure in England – and it pre-dates Paxton's Crystal Palace by three years. Burton and Turner's magnificent Temperate House (overleaf, right), constructed 1862-98, has fruit-filled skyline urns as part of its rich detailing, whereas the more recent Princess of Wales Conservatory (overleaf, bottom left), opened in 1987, has a deceptively simple exterior encasing its sophisticated multi-climate interior. Elsewhere in the gardens, statuary includes decorative urns, heraldic lions and numerous figures.

'*I am at Kew, profiting by the exceptional summer to throw myself wholeheartedly into "plein air" studies in this wonderful garden of Kew. Oh! My dear friend, what trees! what lawns! what undulations of the ground.*'

Camille Pissarro, on his visit to London, 1892

'*. . . there are several of our important Colonies which owe whatever prosperity they possess to the knowledge and experience of, and the assistance given by, the authorities at Kew Gardens. Thousands of letters pass every year between the authorities at Kew and the Colonies, and they are able to place at the service of these colonies not only the best advice and experience, but seeds and samples of economic plants capable of cultivation in the colonies.*'

Joseph Chamberlain, speech in the House of Commons, 1895

OSTERLEY PARK

Osterley Park is one of Robert Adam's three greatest surviving works in London. The other two are Syon House and Kenwood House. Each is a sophisticated, extravagant remodelling of an existing building, and all belong to the early period of Adam's practice. The first two he began working on in 1761; the last, three years later.

At Osterley, Adam took the Elizabethan house, kept the corner towers, and designed a radically modern Palladian mansion. In the grand Ionic double portico (above) that screened the original courtyard, he skilfully blended ideas from at least three Classical buildings to create something fresh. He was inspired by the Portico of Septimus Severus in Rome, the propyleum of the Temple of the Sun at Palmyra and, for the Ionic volutes of the columns, the Erechtheum on the Acropolis. Horace Walpole, an arbiter of classical taste, considered the entrance to be 'as noble as the Propyleum at Athens'. A frieze of a Roman marriage decorates the pediment, while eagles (right) flank the stairway. Osterley was given to the National Trust in 1949.

'... the palace of palaces ... so improved and enriched that all the Percies and Seymours of Sion must die of envy ... here is a double portico that fills the space between the [old] towers of the front ... There is a hall, library, breakfast-room, eating-room, all chefs-d'oeuvre of Adam, a gallery one hundred and thirty feet long, and a drawing-room worthy of Eve before the Fall.'

Horace Walpole, letter to the Countess of Upper Ossery, 21 June 1773

CHISWICK

The fastidious and influential aristocrat Lord Burlington
was patron, promoter and high priest of English
Palladianism for a generation. He had studied Andrea
Palladio's buildings on his trip to Italy in 1714-5, and his
interest was consolidated on his return by the architect
Colen Campbell, who completed Burlington's conversion
to Palladianism and went on to remodel Burlington House
on Piccadilly.

Chiswick House (right) is Burlington's own design, built
from scratch as a Palladian villa on English fields west of
London. William Kent, Burlington's protégé, was consulted
on decoration. And Kent, with Alexander Pope and royal
gardener Charles Bridgeman, who both worked on Marble
Hill House, contributed to the garden. But the house is
essentially Burlington's idea of Palladianism: a return to
the architecture of antiquity as explained and illustrated
by Palladio, avoiding any mannerisms.

It was Burlington's obsessive concern with absolute
Classical standards which gave Chiswick House both its
precision and its dryness. He filled it with his finest art,
used it as a venue to entertain his cultured clique, and
moved there permanently in 1734. A later owner, the
Duchess of Devonshire, held public breakfasts there each
Saturday when she was in residence. Guests would arrive
around three o'clock, feast on lamb, veal, prawns,
strawberries and cherries, then rise around five o'clock
to walk the gardens and boat on the lake.

Near by, the Thameside houses of Chiswick Mall
(overleaf) include Walpole House. Believed to have been
the home of one of Charles II's mistresses, the Duchess of
Cleveland, it was later the fictional setting for the famous
opening scene in William Makepeace Thackeray's *Vanity
Fair*, in which Mr Sedley's carriage drives up to the great
iron gate of Miss Pinkerton's academy for young ladies.

THE HOOVER FACTORY

In the 1930s, factories in the United States and continental Europe were given a proud, palatial and glamorous status. When their influence spread to England, one of the most dramatic to be built was the Hoover factory. Its location on Western Avenue, a main artery in and out of London, quickly made it the landmark it has remained. This was the intention of its American owners, who employed architects Wallis Gilbert and Partners to build the showpiece factory in 1932-5 as part of the promotion of their new machine – the vacuum cleaner.

Unlike other factories, whose dramatic façades hid depressing traditional workfloors, the Hoover factory was designed to dignify the workplace. The richly decorated and colourful entrance (left) was new to England, as was the high-ceilinged, well-lit workers' canteen. The Western Avenue façade, whose window divisions have the grandeur of Classical columns, looked to recent European buildings for inspiration. These included Erich Mendelsohn's Einstein Tower in Potsdam for some of the windows, Josef Hoffmann's Palais Stoclet in Brussels for the decorative bands of red and blue tiles set in white stucco (right), and Charles Rennie Mackintosh's Glasgow School of Art for the fine iron gates.

A HINDU TEMPLE

The beehive-shaped roofs and domes of Shri Swaminarayan Mandir, dedicated in August 1995, rise above the surrounding houses of Neasden in north-west London. The temple is the first of its kind to be built in Europe. In its plan, scale, construction and riot of elaborate carving, it follows the traditional form of the Hindu temple that was developed by the great empires of India during the seventh to twelfth centuries.

The building process was a remarkable feat. No modern materials, such as steel, were used. Rather, 2,775 tons (2,820 tonnes) of Bulgarian limestone and 1,968 tons (2,000 tonnes) of Italian Carrara marble were shipped to India, where 1,500 craftsmen worked on it at twelve sites. Once completed, the 26,300 precision-cut and carved pieces were packed up and sent to London, where they were assembled in the traditional manner, like a giant jigsaw.

The project took three years to complete. More than a thousand volunteers joined the workforce to realize the dream of Pujya Pramakh Swami Maharaj, the high priest and fifth spiritual successor to Shri Swaminarayan to whom the temple is dedicated. Beneath the seven pinnacles and six domes, the marble prayer hall can hold 2,500 people. Although most are part of London's substantial Hindu population, whose parents and grandparents arrived in the 1950s and 1960s from the sub-continent and east Africa, visitors of all denominations are welcome. The adjoining Community Centre, which contains a permanent exhibition on Hinduism, is built of Burmese teak and English oak. The Centre displays yet another Indian skill, even more ancient than stone-carving: the carving of wood into intricate floral designs.

FROM BATTERSEA TO SOUTHWARK AND GREENWICH

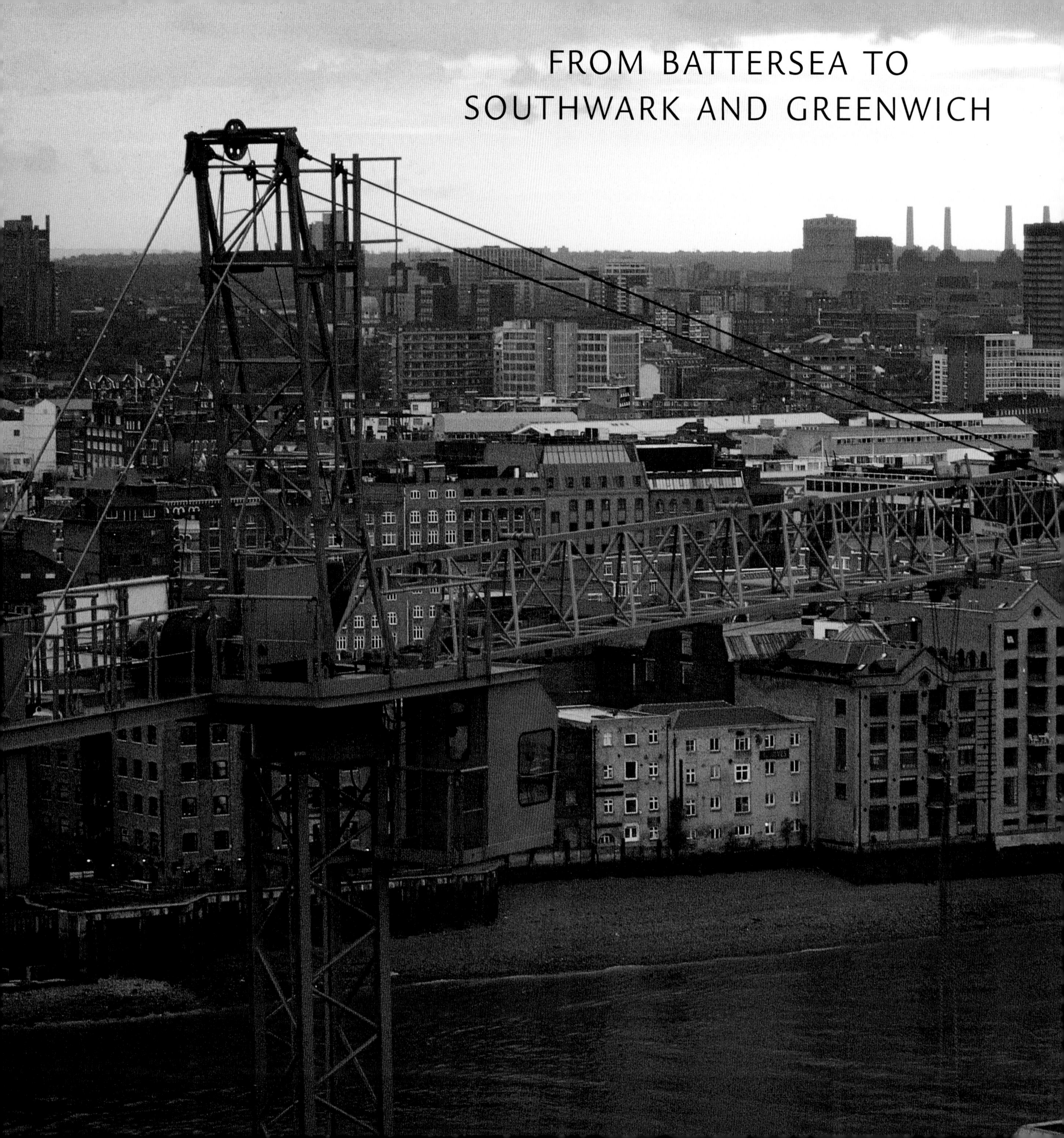

THE SOUTH BANK

'London in the dawn is a clean, unwritten page. You lean over the bridge and know that, in a few hours, the streets will be full of noise and people ... and you feel that, in some way, all the things which people will be discussing in the next dusk are now locked up in this calm greyness ... It is now light. In the east there comes a pink flush low in the sky. The sun has risen. It is a smouldering, short-lived pinkness ... The colour changes, the pink clouds fade into the grey. The cross above St Paul's is gold. The street lights go out ... Over the bridges sounds the rumble of wheels. London, the most masculine city in the world, seems standing clean and stripped, like a boxer entering a ring, for another twenty-four rounds with Fate.'

When H.V. Morton's words were first published in 1926, in *The Nights of London*, although he described the dawn scene as beautiful, the capital was not in good shape. During the horrific First World War of 1914-18, it had suffered bombs and food shortages, and in the aftermath there were docks lying idle, high unemployment and a chronic need for housing. Its sorry state was compounded by the Second World War of 1939-45, which brought devastation to London. The Blitz demolished a third of the City, many docks and the House of Commons. Big Ben survived, though, and its chimes helped to keep British spirits up.

Despite everything, when the war ended in 1945, London was still one of the world's great cities in terms of wealth and political and military influence. But post-war austerity hit the capital hard. Large areas needed rebuilding and priority was given to housing and offices. Food rations would continue until 1953. As Empire dissolved into Commonwealth, hundreds of thousands of people from overseas chose to take up their option of British citizenship. They arrived in London, often moving into housing left empty by people who had moved to the more salubrious suburbs.

From the Monument, completed in 1677, a good panorama of the south bank may be seen (previous page). The Queen's Walk on the south bank (left), faces across to the City on the north bank.

Londoners urgently needed to be cheered up. The answer was to give them a festival. So in 1951, the centenary of the Great Exhibition, the government staged the Festival of Britain. The aim was to show off Britain's new achievements in the realms of science, art and society. The result was a miniature wonderland.

At its heart was a host of temporary stands and buildings constructed on derelict land on the Thames' south bank opposite Westminster. The Dome of Discovery was the largest dome ever constructed, while the silvery aluminium Skylon appeared to be suspended in mid-air. There were also sculptures by Henry Moore, and the thoroughly modern Royal Festival Hall – the festival's only permanent building. Upstream, in the Festival Pleasure Gardens in Battersea Park, there were more amusements; downstream, an exhibition entitled 'Living Architects' in the East End, included visits to the new Lansbury Estate in bombed-out Poplar, where high standards of comfort represented the ideal estate of the future. In all, the whole event was a showcase for the better world that Britain had fought for during the war.

The Festival of Britain was the inspiration for the South Bank Centre – now Europe's largest permanent arts complex. It also kick-started post-war architecture and design, and marked the rebirth of the whole of the south bank from Battersea Park to Greenwich. This process was to gather pace in 1981, when parts of the south bank to the east of the City were included in the government's Enterprise Zone, launched to revive Docklands. Today, other long-forgotten sites are being given new life. One, at Greenwich, is the site for Britain's official millennium celebrations. Here, echoing the 1951 temporary Dome of Discovery, the vast and permanent Millennium Dome designed by Richard Rogers Partnership has a floor area of 20 acres (8 hectares) and a circumference of 1,099 yards (1.5 km).

The key to the original development of London's south bank lay in the bridges and tunnels over and under the Thames, mostly built during the nineteenth century as London mushroomed. Over the years, they have determined how the south bank has developed. With little river transport today other than tourist boats, these are the vital links with the north bank. But these old bridges and tunnels are not enough for today's busy south bank. Already, Hungerford footbridge – completed in 1864 and still an important pedestrian link between Trafalgar Square and the south bank arts complex – is being remodelled by architects Lifschutz Davidson. There are also plans for London to have a new span over the Thames: a footbridge between St Paul's steps and Bankside, designed by Foster and Caro. Perhaps less realistic are the dreams for a 'living bridge' – one incorporating housing – across the Thames. Seven architects competed in a design competition, of which the joint winners were Zaha Hadid architects and Antoine Grumbach and Associates.

Three Victorian bridges, Battersea (1866-90) Chelsea (1851-8) and Albert (1871-3), link Chelsea to Battersea and Wandsworth. On the south bank, the area between Chelsea and Albert bridges is Battersea Park, created in 1853 for the people of London. The marshy land here was raised and filled with the earth dug out during the creation of Victoria Dock. Having been London's centre for the Victorian craze of cycling – forbidden in Hyde Park – its gardens and Henry Moore sculptures lured eight million visitors during the Festival of Britain. Today's more tranquil joggers and Chelsea dog-walkers can enjoy Henry Moore's *Three Standing Figures* and London's first monument dedicated entirely to peace – the London Peace Pagoda – completed in 1985. Meanwhile, nearby redundant Battersea Power Station is to become a vast leisure complex.

Downstream, Vauxhall Bridge, first built in 1816 during the Regency, linked Westminster and the developing Grosvenor estates of Belgravia and Pimlico to the highly popular Vauxhall Gardens. These gardens were famous for their dark walks and louche entertainment, which Boswell considered 'peculiarly adapted to the taste of the English nation . . . a mixture of curious show, gay exhibition, musick, vocal and instrumental, not too refined for the general ear'. Vauxhall Gardens finally closed in 1859. Near by, Surrey County Cricket Club has been holding its cricket matches at the Oval Cricket Ground since 1845.

The first Lambeth Bridge was built in 1861, a century after the closure of Lambeth horse ferry, which had existed since the early sixteenth century. Lambeth Palace, the official residence of the Archbishops of Canterbury since the twelfth century, stands beside the bridge. In 1633, as he moved into the palace, Archbishop Laud's belongings overloaded the ferry so much that it sank. Today, the south end of the bridge has fine views of the Houses of Parliament's river façade, while beside Lambeth Palace the Tradescant Trust's Museum of Garden History maintains the cultural interest of the south bank with its replica of a seventeenth-century garden, filled with plants known to Charles I's gardeners, John Tradescant and his son John.

*'Gilbert walked as far as
the middle of [Lambeth
Bridge] . . . The church bells
kept up their clangorous
discord, softened at times
by the wind. A steamboat
came fretting up the stream;
when it had passed under
the bridge, its spreading
track caught the reflected
gleams and flung them
away to die on
unsearchable depths.'*

George Gissing, *Thyrza*, 1887

*The present Lambeth Bridge
was built in 1929-32. The ancient
crossing from Westminster to
Lambeth was by a ferry that
could carry a coach and horses –
a rarity even in London.
When Westminster Bridge opened
in 1750, the ferry closed.*

'I went along Battersea Bridge,
and thence by a wondrous path across
coq fields, mud ditches, river
embankments . . . wondrous enough
in the darkening dusk . . .'

Thomas Carlyle, *Letters from Chelsea*, 1841

BRIDGES AND POWER STATIONS

Battersea Bridge (left, seen in the background) was originally built of wood in 1771. The only bridge between Westminster and Putney, it boosted the area and was later depicted in James Whistler's moody paintings of the Thames. With the Victorian expansion of London, and the increase of traffic pouring in and out of the capital, more bridges over the Thames were needed. The old Battersea Bridge, demolished in 1881, was replaced by Sir Joseph Bazalgette's cast-iron one in 1886-90. Meanwhile, R.M. Ordish's Albert Bridge (left, seen in the foreground) provided another crossing from Chelsea to Battersea. Built in 1871-3, it combined the cantilever and suspension systems to create a 'straight-link suspension' bridge, each half supported by sixteen straight wrought-iron bars radiating from the top of the cast-iron towers.

Power stations were late additions to the the Thames, joining hundreds of warehouses, wharves, steps, piers and quays strung along its busy banks. Following Chelsea's Lots Road Power Station, opened in 1905, Battersea Power Station (right) opened in 1937. It was designed by Giles Gilbert Scott, architect of the new Waterloo Bridge (1939-45) and, later, of Bankside Power Station (1963) at Southwark. Originally built with two chimneys, it was later doubled in size. Today, purified white vapour no longer billows out of its soaring chimneys and the building is to become an entertainment centre.

A dramatic shaft of light descends on to the Royal Festival Pier (above), built for the 1951 Festival of Britain. Beyond it, Terry Farrell's floodlit Embankment Place dominates the skyline. Built in 1987-90, it suspends 38,000 square yards (32,000 sq. m) of office space above Charing Cross Station, using giant bowstring arches supported on equally enormous columns.

The concrete balconies of Sir Denys Lasdun's Royal National Theatre (left), completed in 1977, offer spectacular views downstream to St Paul's Cathedral. Near by, the Oxo beefstock company built their headquarters (right) in the 1930s. To beat the local ban on illuminated advertisements, they incorporated their logo into back-lit window frames.

THE SOUTH BANK

Westminster Bridge, central London's second bridge, was opened in 1750. Together with Waterloo Bridge and the Hungerford footbridge, it links the south bank arts complex with West End theatreland. The south bank complex started with the Royal Festival Hall in 1951, followed by the National Film Theatre (1958). The smaller concert halls, the Queen Elizabeth Hall and the Purcell Room, were opened in 1967. Next came the Hayward Gallery (1968), the Royal National Theatre (1967-77) with its three stages, and then the Museum of the Moving Image (1988), known affectionately as MOMI.

The area has had a long association with the arts. It was in Waterloo, behind the railway station, that the Old Vic Theatre opened in 1818 as the Royal Coburg Theatre, 'a house of melodrama'. Here, in 1914, Lilian Baylis inaugurated London's first season of Shakespeare plays at reasonable prices, while from 1963 to 1976, the Old Vic was the temporary home of the National Theatre, originally under the direction of Sir Laurence Olivier. In 1982, a Canadian company bought the theatre and refurbished it, and fifteen years later Sir Peter Hall made the Old Vic his company's resident theatre.

Not far away, the Young Vic provides fringe theatre, the Imperial War Museum displays war art and war machines, while part of the riverside County Hall, the former offices of the Greater London Council, houses the London Aquarium, opened in 1997 to display the wonders of the world's oceans and rivers. In the midst of the area, Eurostar's trains began running in 1994 from beneath the glazed bowstring arches of Nicholas Grimshaw and Partners' bold Waterloo International Station, providing a three-and-a-half-hour ride through the Eurotunnel to Paris and Brussels.

When the Queen celebrated her Silver Jubilee in 1977, a generation after the Festival of Britain, a 10-mile- (16-km-) long government-funded London Silver Jubilee Walkway was created around inner London. The riverside stretch from Lambeth to Tower Bridge dips inland only where necessary and provides spectacular views of Westminster, the City and Docklands. The widest pathway is the tree-studded area in front of the south bank complex, where roller-bladers zip between street musicians and second-hand-book sellers. The Walkway then goes inland a little by the landmark Oxo tower, restored by architects Lifschutz Davidson and now home to de luxe rooftop restaurants, shops and designers' studios. It re-emerges beyond Blackfriars Bridge into quite a different area that stretches to London Bridge.

Southwark, opposite the City, was originally a Roman suburb and the site of a Roman garrison. Later it was swallowed into the see of the Bishop of Winchester. Today, one single tantalizing window survives from the bishops' medieval riverside palace that once stood in a 70-acre (28-hectare) park next to Southwark Cathedral, a fine thirteenth-century Augustinian priory church, heavily restored in the nineteenth century.

Southwark was known for its 'houses of prelates, pleasure resorts, prisons and inns'. The George Inn, in nearby Borough High Street, is a galleried coaching inn, a rare survivor of the sort of inn from which Chaucer's pilgrims might have started their journey to Canterbury. Such inns were also used for performing plays. Until Tudor times, theatre consisted either of religious plays or of performances given by bands of actors in the yard of a coaching inn or in a private house or hall. When theatre was banned in the City in 1574, James Burbage built an inn-shaped theatre at Shoreditch. He later moved both company and theatre to be near the Rose, Swan and Hope Theatres at Bankside in Southwark, among the bear-baiting rings and plentiful taverns and prostitutes. Some of Shakespeare's plays were first performed at Burbage's Globe Theatre, which has recently been rebuilt. The ban on theatre was lifted after the Restoration, yet when Pepys went to the Theatre Royal Drury Lane in 1666, he was still 'in mighty pain lest I should be seen by anybody to be at a play'. Later, Henry Fielding's crude satires at Nash's Haymarket Theatre caused the Lord Chamberlain to reintroduce powers of censorship in 1737 which were lifted only in 1968.

Southwark's recent triumph is the transformation of Giles Gilbert Scott's redundant Bankside Power Station into the home of the Tate Gallery's International Collection of Modern Art. Behind it soars Manhattan Loft Company's dramatic warehouse apartments. These,

linked to the north bank with a new pedestrian bridge, will, more than anything else, revive Southwark's ancient importance in London.

The south bank area between streamlined London Bridge and idiosyncratic Tower Bridge quickly benefited from the Docklands development initiative of the 1980s. Already it feels established. Converted warehouses stretching along Shad Thames and new developments such as Piers Gough's The Circle provide offices and homes, while the streets and river walks are furnished with new sculptures. There are restaurants, shops, the London Dungeon for children and the riverside Design Museum. There is also London's only surviving ferry, which runs between the battleship HMS *Belfast*, moored near Tower Bridge, and the Tower of London.

A little way from the river is Bermondsey, with street names such as Tanner Street and Morocco Street revealing its origins as London's old leather-working area. Some sixteenth-century houses survive in and around Bermondsey Street and Bermondsey Square. Here early risers can enjoy the beauty of London at dawn as described by Morton, while they pick up bargains at the antiques market.

Downriver, Rotherhithe's many piers evoke trading memories, as do the isolated pubs that once served sailors and adventurers, pirates and gamblers. There are no bridges here, but in 1843 the world's first under-river public thoroughfare was opened, the Thames Tunnel. Designed by Marc Brunel, it enabled dock-workers living at Rotherhithe to walk to their work at Wapping. This footpath is now part of the London Underground. The revival of Rotherhithe near the site of Edward III's palace and the Pilgrims' Mayflower pub includes the restoration of the 1843 Thames Tunnel Mills.

Further downstream, sweeping round the curving Thames past Surrey Docks, Deptford's late eighteenth-century Albany Street and its cluster of piers testify to the area's naval and trading status.

The delicate stone tracery of a rose window (above), possibly dating to 1109, miraculously survives from Winchester Palace, huddled among the buildings of Southwark. In neighbouring Bermondsey, the extravagantly finished theatrical apartments of The Circle (right), designed by Piers Gough of CZWG Architects in 1987-9, have diagonal glazing bars and cobalt-blue painted bricks.

'After dinner on the 21st of September, at about two o'clock, I went with my companions over the water, and in the strewn roof-house saw the tragedy of the first Emperor Julius ... very well acted ... And thus every day at two o'clock in the afternoon in the city of London two and sometimes three comedies are performed at separate places ... The places are so built that they play on a raised platform, and everyone can well see it all ... And in the pauses of the comedy, food and drink are carried round amongst the people.'

Thomas Platter, 1599, quoted in
E.K. Chambers, *The Elizabethan Stage*

THE GLOBE THEATRE

In 1599, James Burbage moved his Globe Theatre to Bankside in Southwark, where it quickly outshone the Rose and Swan theatres and staged first performances of Shakespeare's *Hamlet*, *Othello*, *King Lear* and *Macbeth*. Rebuilt after a fire, plays by Beaumont and Fletcher, Heywood, Middleton and Webster were performed before the theatre was closed and demolished in 1644.

The reconstruction of the Globe Theatre (left), part of the south bank's revival as a riverside entertainment centre, was the dream of Sam Wanamaker, realized by Pentagram Design. Work began in 1987. Contemporary illustrations and archaeological evidence were consulted. Then, using traditional materials and techniques, the polygonal building of twenty three-storey wooden bays was built, and thatched with Norfolk reed. In 1997, the new Globe staged its first performance.

*'One goes down the widening reaches
through a monstrous variety of
shipping, great steamers, great sailing
ships, trailing the flags of all the world,
a monstrous confusion of lighters,
witches' conferences of brown-sailed
barges, wallowing lugs, a tumultuous
crowding and jostling of cranes . . .'*

H.G. Wells, *Tono-Bungay*, 1909

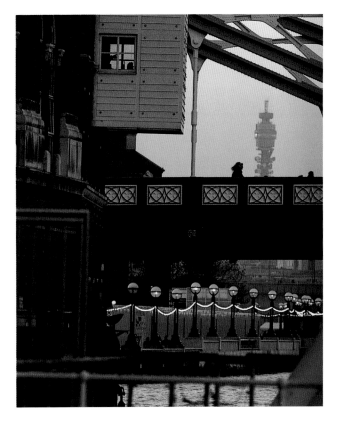

WHARVES AND WAREHOUSES

The Port of London is silent today. But the countless piers, stairs, wharves and warehouses lining its banks bear witness to past commotion, especially in this stretch of river, the Pool of London. Horace Jones designed Tower Bridge (left), built in 1886-94. It is London's only bridge downstream of London Bridge. Visually it matches the medieval Tower of London, yet its Victorian engineering enables it to open for tall shipping. Its engineer, John Wolfe-Barry, constructed the stone-clad towers in steel to support the bascules and contain lifts up to the footbridge.

Beside the southern end of Tower Bridge, the Bermondsey warehouses have been revived with notable success. Conran Roche have transformed the seventeen protected buildings of the Butler's Wharf complex (right, above) from spice warehouses and offices for rice, corn and flour merchants into homes, offices, restaurants and industrial workshops. Next to it, CZWG Architects's China Wharf (1988) (right, below) provides apartments with jolly river façades. Behind this peaceful riverside, the Friday morning Bermondsey antiques market (overleaf), also known as the New Caledonian Market, is full of noise and bustle.

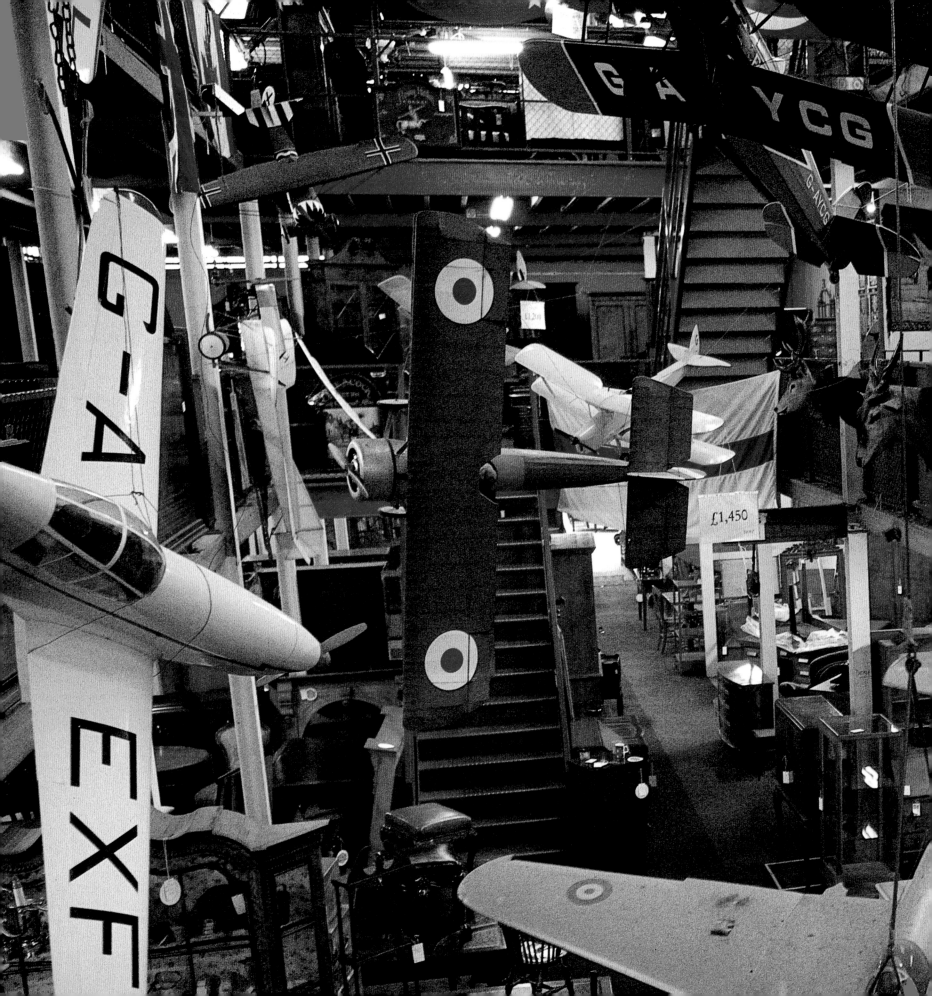

Of London's south bank villages it is only Greenwich that enjoys the combination of spectacular attractions and a link with the north bank of the Thames. Although monarchs abandoned Greenwich in favour of Kensington and Hampton Court, its royal status remained. Inigo Jones's Queen's House, completed in 1635 and England's first Palladian villa, stands centre stage. Around it are grouped Wren's Royal Naval College and his Flamsteed House at the Old Observatory. Today, these form part of the National Maritime Museum, the world's largest maritime museum.

It was the local shipping business and the hospital – as well as the hilly site – that attracted the wealthy to Greenwich in the eighteenth century. They built fine houses in Greenwich itself or up the hill on the 260 acres (100 hectares) of Blackheath – one of which is Ranger's House, built in 1710 and now a gallery of paintings.

Greenwich has always been in close touch with the City and its merchants – and not just by river. London's first railway opened in 1836, linking Greenwich and London Bridge. The Greenwich Foot Tunnel was opened in 1902 to replace the ferry and to enable workers to walk to the docks to the north. More recently, computer-controlled trains on the Docklands Light Railway, opened in 1987, skim past Canary Wharf Tower and across the redeveloped Docklands to Island Gardens, right beside the entrance to the foot tunnel.

Wren, who watched St Paul's being built from his Bankside home, would cross the river by boat to Island Gardens to enjoy the view of his Greenwich buildings. H.V. Morton surely knew this view, but would probably have enjoyed the one from Greenwich Park even more: the sweeping view of the Docklands, the City's cluster of towers, the dome of St Paul's and, upriver around a curve in the Thames, the pinnacles of the Houses of Parliament and the tower of Big Ben, all of them at dawn 'standing clean and stripped, like a boxer entering a ring, for another twenty-four rounds with Fate'.

Mature horse chestnut trees line an avenue in Greenwich Park. Charles II brought order and formality to the rough hills at Greenwich enjoyed by Tudor kings. He invited André Le Nôtre, who designed the park at Versailles, to create this and other avenues, although the intended focus – the Royal Observatory – followed a decade later, to designs by Sir Christopher Wren. Many of the park's trees – including the chestnuts, paper birches, caster-oil trees and some cypresses – survive from Le Nôtre's planting or earlier.

THE SOUTH BANK

GREENWICH

Ocean-racing boats skim along the Thames at Greenwich (far left and left, centre), a reminder of the area's key role in Britain's trading and naval history. This viewpoint is alongside the Old Royal Observatory, the historic centre for astronomical and maritime studies. Through it passes the prime meridian of the world.

The fine prospects from here and from Greenwich Hill (left, below) have been favourites with artists and writers since the eighteenth century. Opened in 1705, the park drew locals who impressed Daniel Defoe in the 1720s as being 'a kind of smart Collection of Gentlemen, rather than Citizens, and of being Persons of Quality and Fashion'.

This panorama embraces Inigo Jones's elegant Queen's House and Wren's Royal Naval Hospital, begun in 1695. Across the Thames, the most striking silhouette of the Docklands is Canary Wharf Tower, the centrepiece for Skidmore, Owings & Merrill's massive development, built 1988-91. Designed by Cesar Pelli, it was the first skyscraper to be clad in steel, although it is neither as tall nor as thin as the architect had hoped. Wren's favourite view of his Greenwich buildings is believed to have been from the Isle of Dogs, looking across the Thames to his river façade (left, top).

The *Cutty Sark* (right) stands on King William Walk. A tea clipper built in 1869 for a London shipowner, Captain John Willis, and named from a poem by Robert Burns, she beat the world record in 1871 by sailing her cargo from China to England in 107 days. She remained in service until 1922.

LONDON CHRONOLOGY

43 Roman Emperor Claudius invades Britain; establishes port and crossing at Londinium.

61 Boudicca, queen of the Iceni, burns down Londinium; the Romans rebuild.

200 Romans build a wall around Londinium, with seven gates; Romans stay until 410.

604 The first St Paul's Cathedral and St Peter's (later the site of Westminster Abbey) founded.

1016 Danish Viking, Canute, proclaimed King of all England; makes London his capital.

1052 Edward the Confessor begins building Westminster Abbey; Westminster becomes a royal seat.

1066 William the Conqueror wins the Battle of Hastings; Normans rule until 1154.

1070s William I begins building the Tower of London, a defence against the City's merchants.

1154 Henry II initiates Plantagenet rule, which lasts until 1399.

1176 Wooden London Bridge rebuilt in stone: London's only bridge until 1750.

1192 Henry FitzAilwin becomes the first mayor of London.

1197 City wins lucrative management of the Thames; the river reverts to Crown in 1857.

1215 King John signs Magna Carta; City wins independent status from Westminster.

1348-50 London's population of 50,000 ravaged by Black Death (bubonic plague).

1399 Henry IV initiates Lancastrian rule which lasts until 1461.

1461 Edward IV initiates Yorkist rule which lasts until 1485.

1477 William Caxton publishes the first book printed in England.

1485 Henry VII initiates Tudor rule which lasts until 1603; population of London is about 75,000.

1529 Cardinal Wolsey falls; Henry VIII acquires Whitehall and Hampton Court Palaces.

1532-4 Henry VIII breaks with the Church of Rome, to become head of the Church of England.

1536 Dissolution of the Monasteries begins; 800 closed by 1540.

1566 Royal Exchange founded; London soon outstrips Amsterdam in trading.

1574 Theatres banned from the City; Bankside becomes London's entertainment centre.

1603 James VI of Scotland becomes James I of England, initiating Stuart rule.

1631 Inigo Jones designs London's first square, the Piazza in Covent Garden.

1637 Charles I opens Hyde Park, the first public royal park.

1649 Charles I beheaded; Oliver Cromwell presides over the Commonwealth, then Protectorate.

1660 Restoration of the monarchy; Charles II revives Stuart rule which lasts until 1714.

1666 Great Fire of London destroys four-fifths of the City.

1675 Sir Christopher Wren begins building the new St Paul's Cathedral.

1689 William and Mary move to Kensington Palace, one of the sovereign's London homes until 1762.

1700 London's population is about 575,000, making it western Europe's biggest city.

1714 George I initiates Hanoverian rule which lasts until present day (name of royal family changed to Windsor in 1917).

1725-53 Grosvenor Square laid out, the centrepiece of the Grosvenors' Mayfair development.

1750 Westminster Bridge, London's second bridge, opens.

1762 George III and Queen Charlotte move into Buckingham House (later renamed Buckingham Palace).

1801 First London population census: 959,000 (128,000 in the City).

1802 London is the world's largest port; first enclosed docks opened.

1811-17 Waterloo Bridge is built, the first of fourteen bridges over the Thames to be built, or rebuilt, this century.

1829 John Nash completes the laying out of Regent Street, Regent's Park and Regent's Canal.

1829 Metropolitan Police force founded; public horse-drawn bus service begins.

1834 Palace of Westminster (Houses of Parliament) burn down; rebuilding starts 1835.

1836 London Bridge–Greenwich railway opens, one of fourteen railway termini built this century.

1837 Queen Victoria, aged eighteen, accedes to the throne; rules sixty-four years until her death in 1901.

1851 The Great Exhibition held in Hyde Park; South Kensington museums built as a result.

1863 The world's first underground railway service opens, from Paddington to King's Cross.

1890 The first 'Tube' train runs, using electric trains in deep-level tunnels.

1901 Population of Greater London is 6,506,000; will peak at 10 million in 1930s and 1940s.

1939-45 Second World War; Blitz bombings destroy a third of City of London and many docks.

1951 Festival of Britain; south bank arts complex built as a result.

1967 Civic Amenities Act passed; within twenty years, 300 areas of London protected from uncontrolled development.

INDEX

ACKNOWLEDGMENTS

For permission to reprint copyright material the author and the Publishers would like to thank the following:

ARNOLD BENNETT: from *Imperial Palace* (reprinted by permission of A.P. Watt Ltd on behalf of The Literary Executors of Arnold Bennett). CAROL KENNEDY: from *Mayfair, a Social History* (Century Hutchinson Ltd). OSBERT LANCASTER: from *All Done from Memory* (John Murray Ltd). JESSICA MITFORD: from *Hons and Rebels* (Victor Gollancz Ltd). H.V. MORTON: from 'The Nights of London' in *H.V. Morton's London* (Methuen). NIKOLAUS PEVSNER: from *The Buildings of England: London: Volume I* (Penguin Books Ltd). DORA RUSSELL: from *The Tamarisk Tree* (Virago). RAPHAEL SAMUEL: from *The Saving of Spitalfields* by Mark Girouard (The Spitalfields Trust). MICHAEL WHARTON: from *The Stretchford Chronicles* (copyright © Michael Wharton. Extract from an article which first appeared in The Daily Telegraph). H.G. WELLS: from *Tono-Bungay* (reprinted by permission of A.P. Watt Ltd on behalf of The Literary Executors of the Estate of H.G. Wells).

Every effort has been made to contact or trace all copyright holders. The Publishers will be glad to make good any errors or omissions brought to their attention in future editions.

Map of London © Collins 1997. Reproduced with permission of HarperCollins Cartographic. MM-0298-100.

The Publishers are grateful to Anne Askwith and Ruth Carim for assistance in creating the book, and to Helen Smith for the index.

Editors Caroline Bugler, Hilary Mandleberg
Editorial Assistant Tom Windross
Production Liz Stewart
Head of Pictures Anne Fraser
Art Director Caroline Hillier
Editorial Director Erica Hunningher